CW01651656

A Practical Guide to Off-grid Living in Alaska

Copyright 2019 Jon Crocker
All photos and diagrams property of the author

Table of Contents

Introduction

You are not alone.

There are countless others that feel lost in modern life. Thousands that want to slow things down, simplify, breathe clean air. It's been that way for a while. This isn't the first "back to the land" movement. They've been happening predictably—cyclically—for generations, as we wonder what our parents saw in suburbia. They saw opportunity for us. They saw a future that promised the impossible. They saw ease. Comfort. Security. As those promises slowly fade, we turn back to the land. The land has always been able to provide for those willing to work with it.

Alaska is different. To successfully live close to the land in Alaska requires unique skills, superhuman patience, specialized knowledge, determination, luck, a streak of madness, and optimistic idiocy. Or you could just have a whole lot of money and a helicopter to fly all of your gear out into the bush. But someone with that kind of money doesn't need this book. They hire consultants. They spend $50,000 on their solar power system.

For those that can't afford a private helicopter, you have me—the guy who makes do with a $3000 solar power system. You have me and reality TV, and I'm going to be a lot more honest with you than reality TV is. We've been there and done that—tried and failed at doing it in the wilderness with little more than hand tools. Lived in remote villages. Lived off-grid in a backcountry cabin miles down a footpath. Now I'm older, fatter, and smarter. We see neighbors come and go. Singles and couples and families all trying to do the off-grid Alaska homestead thing—and failing for various reasons.

I'm tired of seeing people fail. You have the benefit of my failures and theirs.

In fact, my wife suggested that this book should be called "How not to give up after six months." Because most people with Alaskan dreams give up in under two years (and yes, some in as few as six months). Off-grid homesteading in Alaska is not an easy thing to do.

The bigger issue is that of expectations: people expect one thing and find another. They find that it's not going to be the way they'd imagined it in their dreams. It's not going to be the way you see on reality TV. In some ways, it's a lot less attractive. But in other ways, it's better. A lot better.

You need to know what to expect so that you don't get disappointed.

The title of this book is a misnomer. It's hardly possible to live off-grid in Alaska in a very practical way. You will be torn between two worlds. Most of your time will be spent in the wild beauty that draws many of us to Alaska. But you will have to go to town for gas. For propane. For work. Yes, you'll need money, and that usually requires work. For groceries (did you really think you'd be able to get by with just wild meat and berries?). For going to the bank and paying bills and maybe even visiting the hospital because you aren't as handy with that splitting maul as you thought you were. And that's okay. It still beats the lower 48 urban commute.

Or you could ignore my advice. That's okay as well. Alaska isn't for everyone. And for those of us that like it this way, we don't mind when people have that "getting-the-hell-out-of-Alaska" moving sale. We get great deals. People even give stuff away. I've gotten free propane tanks, fancy grills, construction materials, tools, clothes, and even super-expensive sleeping bags good to -20 degrees Fahrenheit. All stuff that people thought they were going to need to make their Alaskan dreams come true. The truth is that "stuff" is the least of your worries. You can't *buy* success in Alaska by having the right gear. What is far more important is what is inside your head: knowledge. Attitude. Creativity. And, most importantly, the ability to connect with your community. That might seem counterintuitive, as most people seem to move here to escape the crowds. But these aren't crowds. These are your neighbors, and you won't make it without them.

In this book you'll find how-tos. You'll find tips. You'll find anecdotes meant to illustrate important points. You'll find philosophy, which is just as important as anything else (changing the way you think will take time). You'll also find far too many poop jokes.

This book is everything I wish I had known before I began—and more. It is the result of my experience, my research, my conversations with people who have been here a lot longer. It isn't meant to replace construction manuals or wild plant identification guides, but rather to work *with* them. The idea is to integrate all of it into something easy-to-read.

So, if you'd like to give Alaska a try, and if you'd like to be successful, please read on. We could always use a good neighbor.

Acknowledgments

We weren't always experts on these things. We still aren't. But we wouldn't have gotten this far without the help and expertise of many people. In particular, we'd like to thank three people that have taught us more than any others: Mark Vachavake, Matt Trail, and Glen Fuller. It's not just their experience that is valuable: it is their patience and desire to teach.

Author's Note:

Measurements in this book are given in units commonly used in America (Fahrenheit, miles, and so on). My apologies to those used to the metric system.

Chapter One: Buying Land

Most people start their Alaskan adventure with the purchase of land. This is a bad idea. You should probably try living in Alaska first—learning what you need to know before you need to know it—and then get some land. But you'll still need to buy some eventually. You can try borrowing land, but most people will be reticent to loan you any if you aren't going to return it in the same condition (and you'll have to poop *somewhere*, making it unlikely you'll return it in the same condition). Historically, some have stolen land very successfully, but that usually requires military enforcement. If you happen to have your own personal army, then your time might be better spent invading a small country that you can have all to yourself—maybe French Guiana. France isn't even on the same continent, and they don't pay much attention to that particular possession. You might be able to do it late at night without anyone noticing.

Most parcels of land in Alaska cost less than what it would take to feed an army, so just buy some land already.

But *buyer beware*.

If you aren't familiar with Alaskan soils, vegetation, and landforms, you may not have much of an idea of what you are actually buying, or if you can even get to it without owning your own aircraft. The two main issues are access and "buildable" land.

Access

It's easy to buy land in Alaska. You can just go to the state's Department of Natural Resources webpage, pick a parcel, enter your credit card number, and voila! You've got yourself some Alaska. And it looked very nice in the pictures. But it's the duty of the buyer to verify access. That means you might not actually be able to get to it, or that you can't access it without trespassing on someone else's property. Before submitting that credit card payment, ask yourself the following questions:

Does it have a driveway or parking area? If not, you'll have to park in the road (if there is one), and that might anger people that use that road. Alaskan back roads can be narrow and in poor shape. It's nice to be able to use the whole thing for driving when we can, especially when it's icy.

Does it even have a road? If not, you'll have to park your vehicle nearby and access your property by foot, by 4-wheeler (also known as an ATV), or by snowmachine (what Alaskans call snowmobiles). There *are* off-grid subdivisions in which local residents all park in a particular area and do this—but it leaves your vehicle at the mercy of thieves and bears. If you don't leave anything valuable in your vehicle, that might not be a problem.

Does it have a trail? If you can't drive to it and must park nearby, you'll need to put a trail in (if there isn't one already). Ever broken trail in Alaska? It's not always easy. In some places, the land is firm and grassy—no problem breaking trail there. But sometimes it's full of ruts, it's soggy, full of dense shrubbery, or even thickly wooded.

Speaking of breaking trail, some people from out of state just bought about 8 or 9 contiguous lots in my neighborhood, totaling several dozen acres at least. They were under the impression that there was a road right to the lots. Sure, there is a *platted* road, but that's not the same as an actual road. It just means that there's a space set aside for constructing a road someday. This platted road has to cross about 800 hundred feet off wooded land, 800 more of semi-soggy muskeg, cross over a small stream (know how to build a bridge?), then go up another wooded hill to get to the lots. This road will require various permits and hundreds of thousands of dollars to construct—money that this couple doesn't have. Perhaps they should have visited before they spent all that money buying lots that they can't afford to get to. They'll either have to sell them again or find a place to park and take 4-wheelers in and out.

If a lot doesn't have any hope of nearby vehicle access, you might luck out with river access (if there is a navigable river to it…or at least near it). Some people buy a boat and access their land that way. However, riverfront land tends to be a lot more expensive, and there are often restrictions on what you can build near a river (especially if it is a salmon spawning river).

If there is no hope of road, trail, or river access, you might be able to fly in. A lot of people buy remote land on a lakefront and get dropped off by floatplane. This can work very well—but it is expensive. If you only need two trips per year, it's not so bad. But, as you'll learn, most people need to come in and out of their property more than twice a year. If it costs $1000 or more each time, you might be wishing you'd just stayed in the lower states.

Plane access elsewhere really depends on whether or not there is a suitable place to land. A lot of land that can be easily purchased online is on the soggy side—not suitable for landing a bush plane. Most Alaskans highly recommend getting your boots on the ground before you buy. If you can't do that, you need to be able to read and interpret aerial imagery and plat maps.

Figure 1: You cannot get here by driving. It is 400 miles from the road system.

Geography is your friend

Learning to read plat maps is important because it will tell you all of the legal access points for the lots in a subdivision. Roads will be on the map (though they might not exist yet in real life), and any of these are legal access. There is also access along section lines—and I do know a couple of people that depend on a section line easement for access to their cabins. A plat map will let you know about any other easements or building setbacks.

Aerial imagery can give you insight into the nature of the land. While being there in person (or looking at high-quality photographs) is preferable, aerial imagery might be able to save you from buying land that is too soggy to build on. Google Earth is a great starting point. You can zoom in, change angles, and even overlay a plat map so that you know what your lot will be like.

Tip 1: Look at your location at a near-level angle (street view level, basically, though it probably won't be on a street) to see if it's flat or if it has some higher areas. If it's all flat, that could be a bad sign—it might be all flat because it's technically wetlands. Ideally, you'll want at least some area that is higher than the rest. Google Earth also indicates the elevation at the location of the cursor (look at the very bottom of the window). You can use those numbers to see how much higher one area is compared to another.

Tip 2: Zoom in and look at the vegetation. Are there lots of ponds? That would also be a bad sign (likely wetlands). Standing water also means lots of mosquitoes during the warm season. They aren't very fun. Not for humans, anyway. They're *lots* of fun for swallows. If you're lucky, you might get some swallows during summer. Ideally, you'll want forested or shrubby land—you want soil that is strong enough to support vibrant vegetation. Then it will also be likely to hold your cabin.

Tip 3: Look at historical imagery. Google Earth lets you look back through older aerial imagery (it's a button that looks like a clock). This is useful because you can see what the land might look like at different times of year (depending on how many photographs are available—some very remote areas only have one photograph available!). You might be able to figure out when the snow comes and when it finally melts. You can figure out how long the ice might stay on local river. In my area, it lets me know just which areas were logged in the past and when that logging occurred (if you see that an area *used* to be forested, that's also a good sign—likely good soil, yet you won't have to do any clearing—though the downside is that there won't be as much firewood or building logs available).

Tip 4: Use image overlay to put your plat map onto Google Earth. You'll need to adjust and then make it partially transparent, but it can give you even more insight into what your lot looks like (and a great way to see what your access looks like).

Another great tool is the USDA Web Soil Survey. It's a free online tool that gives you access to soil survey data, which is available for many areas in Alaska (i.e. Anchorage, the Matanuska-Susitna Borough, Kenai Peninsula Borough, Denali Borough, Fairbanks area, Delta Junction area, and more). You simply find your area on their map, select your specific place by drawing a rectangle around it, and then click a button to get soil data (the site itself has tutorials). What it will give you is a map that shows different numbers in different map areas, each number corresponding to a soil type. It gives you a quick guide to each soil type found on the map, and the information can be tremendously helpful: average depth to groundwater, drainage rates, water retention rates, frequency of ponding, soil profile (what you'll find in each layer—i.e. loam, gravel, clay, dead bodies, etc.), and suitability for agriculture. In regards to suitability for agriculture, it has a scale: 1-7, one being best, seven being worst. There are no "grade one" soils in Alaska (not naturally occurring, anyway). There are a couple of places with grade two soils—the Delta Junction area and an area directly west of Anderson (the Kobe agricultural project). Other grade two soils might exist near Palmer, but usually only if they've been in use for a while and are well taken care of. For the most part, you'll be lucky to find grade three soils—these can be turned into grade two soils with some care on your part (if you plan to be a gardener). The web soil survey will tell you if an area is wetlands, also known locally as *muskeg*.

Muskeg

Muskeg is a very broad term. There are many different kinds of muskeg. Some are more useful to people than others, but all types are important habitat and an essential part of an Alaskan ecosystem. They get a bad rap because you can't build on them. If you buy a lot that is nothing but muskeg, that can be an issue. Some types can support structures if you use certain kinds of foundations (like the helical piers mentioned in chapter 2), but in general, you'll need some land that isn't muskeg if you want to live in a permanent dwelling.

One type of muskeg is very grassy, sedgy, and wet—full of ponds or mini-lakes. This type is least useful to most people, but very important as nesting sites for certain birds (some of which are very tasty). It can be impossible to traverse during the warm season.

As muskeg gets drier and higher, it supports plants that are of greater use to us humans:

- Sphagnum moss (also known as peat moss), great as toilet paper, a medium for starting plant seedlings, and as wound dressing material.
- Labrador tea, a medicinal plant (careful not to make it too strong).
- Willow, a source of salicylic acid (also known as "aspirin").
- Blueberry
- Lingonberry
- Crowberry
- Various other berries and medicinal plants (see the chapter on food)

As muskeg transitions to even higher ground, you'll start seeing trees like black spruce and stunted birch. Tree species can be signs as to how wet soils are. While some muskeg is very obvious (it is flat and wet with few to no trees), some areas that looks like high ground might still be quite wet. If you don't see any robust, healthy trees, it is probably soggy. Generally, the more "lush" the vegetation is, the better the soil is. Muskeg is also quite acidic, and only certain plants can tolerate it. Trees that are signs of high, dry ground would be white spruce, aspen, and alder. Signs of muskeg are black spruce, willow, sphagnum moss, and berries. Cottonwoods tend to grow in riparian areas (along streams). Birches can go either way—sometimes they can be on soggy ground, but often they will be found on high ground (especially in larger groves). Again, the best way to judge would be to look at the size and health of the tree.

Anecdote: Our First Alaskan Land

I didn't necessarily want to move to Alaska. It was just one of many options. All I knew is that I wanted to get some land in an un-crowded area—a place where I could live simply. Lots of people want that. I had many reasons for wanting this. Mostly I wanted to stop living a consumer lifestyle. I wanted to be a *producer*. Or maybe a part-time hunter-gatherer. I wanted *out* of the patterns that governed my time (whether I wanted them or not), as if a certain kind of life had been prescribed for me and I had to keep on that prescribed path because there were no other feasible ways to live—even though I knew that there *were* other ways to live. And one of the things I looked for when shopping for land online was some kind of freshwater stream on the property (since we need water in order to survive, and this seemed the simplest way to make sure I had it). That narrowed my options considerably, especially since most cheap and un-crowded land is in the western states, and those states tend to be dry.

I'd been searching on various real estate websites. I'd also been looking on eBay. I would do a search and click the little boxes for my price range and the states I'd be willing to live in, then scan for properties that advertised river or creek frontage. I saw some here and there—many of them only boasting seasonal streams (since the dry season in much of the western U.S. is *really* dry). One property from Alaska popped up—and it fit my budget. It was a bit on the remote side, but still accessible. I went ahead and put a bid on it and didn't think too much about it.

Well, I should have thought about it. The auction ended and I had the highest bid. There was a strange rush of excitement: after months of looking and longing, I had done it. Or eBay had done it for me. I never expected to be the highest bidder, but now I had the choice: do I go through with the deal or just forget about it? Because I still could have backed out of it. The bid only represented the down payment. I'd still have to make payments for the rest, but it wasn't anything I couldn't afford, assuming I kept myself in work for a few years.

My wife (who wasn't yet my wife at this point) was in disbelief. "You just bought land in Alaska? What the hell?!? How are you even going to pay for that?" It was a good question. I was pretty much unemployed at the time (technically self-employed as a musician-slash-substitute teacher) and had no savings to speak of. The property seemed so far off, a dreamland. But the pictures were stunning. And it would be ours if I decided to go ahead and sign what I needed to sign. Which I did. I even went a bit overboard by opting to get title insurance, which was actually a good idea—there turned out to be a lien on the property. The sellers hadn't finished buying it from the state. In fact, that's a good thing to remember: make sure you go through a professional title company when you buy land, especially if it's owner-financed. I know some people who have signed contracts that didn't end up giving them anything but headaches (and certainly didn't give them actual title to the land). There are unscrupulous people out there that are eager to take advantage of someone's dreams.

I had gone about it backwards. Bought land sight-unseen. It was good land, actually. But instead of planning my future around my life as it already existed (which is easier when you already live in Alaska and have a source of income), I had to plan how I was going to make it work. How was I going to *find* work? Because I could barely pay for the land as it was. How was I going to get all of the necessary stuff? How would I transport it to a place that you can't drive to? How would I build in such a place?

The land wasn't as remote as some bush properties can be—only about 20 miles from a decent-sized town (a bush hub—not on the road system). It was on a little bench just above a lake, and what's more, you could drive to the lake from the town. But my land was on the *other* side of the lake, just uphill, and the little stream ran through it and into the lake. And it was a *big* lake. Still, I inspected the land from afar to the best of my abilities (mostly on Google Earth). I planned and I sketched. I designed dozens of potential structures that might have worked. I researched the local area thoroughly. It was great exercise in dreaming and planning.

The reality, though, was that I had been too hasty. I realized that there was no way I'd be able to live in that spot year-round. I'd need to work in the local town, and it would not be possible to commute (a commute would require boating several miles across a lake, then driving a questionable dirt road for many miles before getting to actual pavement, then many more miles of regular pavement). The trip would take the better part of a day. So the plan changed: get a job in the town, then slowly work on the property as we lived and worked in town. But that was also easier said than done: bush hubs have limited work opportunities. Mostly these are limited to healthcare (local clinic or hospital), airlines, and the local school (or schools). Since I'd worked as a substitute teacher (and various other school-related jobs), that seemed like a good place to start. But you can't just call up and get a job. You have to have a teaching certificate. That takes a couple of years.

I found an alternative certification program funded by the state that offered a pretty good deal: you could work toward a certificate while teaching for two years in a "high needs" school (in other words: a bush village). You only needed an endorsable degree, a background check/fingerprints, and to pass an interview. It was a step in the right direction, but the school districts nearest my land were not participants in the program. So the plan changed yet again: work in a different part of Alaska, save money, and then get a job near our land once I had a teaching certificate. We moved to Anchorage in spring for a crash-course job training (student teaching a summer school session) before having most of a summer to spend before we moved to the village where I'd be teaching.

With just enough extra money, we got the idea that we would spend the rest of the summer camping on our lot. So we packed our bags and bought our plane tickets, leaving after a couple of days spent buying gear—two-way radios, a tent, sleeping bags, a rifle with ammunition, and any spare tools we didn't already have. I formulated a rough plan: after getting into town, we'd need to rent a vehicle. I knew there were rental vehicles available. We'd need to buy food. We'd need to buy a few building supplies. We'd need a skiff and a motor and a day or two to cart everything across the lake. After that, it would be up to us to build and browse and explore and learn. It was all very exciting.

And it was a foolish idea. We got into town with two huge backpacks. I also carried a gun case in one hand (with a 30-06). Trying to conserve our money, we walked into the center of town (instead of taking a taxi), which itself was a couple of miles—and very tiring with about 70 pounds on each of our backs. In town I found a phone book. I called the rental car place (the only one in town) and asked to rent a vehicle that could get us to at least the side of the lake. Something with 4-wheel drive and high clearance. They didn't have one. My heart sank. Or at least it felt like it did. All of their vehicles were rented with the exception of one: a little 2-wheel-drive 4-door sedan (there aren't many options in these small towns to begin with). It wasn't exactly something we could use to tow a boat across a mucky road. But we had no choice, so I rented it—we couldn't keep walking everywhere with all of that weight on our backs.

We soon learned how much things can cost in the bush—often double or triple what you'd pay on the road system. We bought food at one of the stores. We bought gas. We went to the hardware store to look at tools and the local bulletin board, and ended up talking with some of the guys there. They were hanging around the way you'd expect they would in a bush town on a lazy summer day. One of them had an outboard motor he'd love to sell me. Another had a lead on a boat and some boating advice. I don't know if they were trying to foist second-rate gear upon me or if they were genuinely trying to be helpful. My experiences suggest the latter. I took down their numbers in case we found a way to transport a boat. But we had to see if we could even drive to the lake first.

We hit the road and headed out of town. The mountains grew near. Our excitement swelled. It was a perfect sunny day, everything greener than any green we'd ever seen. We turned from the pavement onto the winding, narrow road that took us along a mountainside—a road that would keep us on high ground for as long as possible. Then the road dropped down for the final miles, and we came to a stop: it was flooded with spring thaw. We could see the other side of the great puddle (it was actually a small stream overflowing its banks). But we could not see the road beneath the stream. Could not see if there was a little bridge beneath the water we'd need to find with our small tires. Could not tell how deep the water was in the middle. Could not trust a little rented sedan to get us across. Did not want to return a soggy, flooded rental car and have to pay all kinds of damages. So we turned around and drove back up the mountain. From up there, we could *see* it: our land. It was beautiful. It was everything we'd hoped it would be, and it was just beyond our reach—for the moment.

Figure 2: The land that started it all.

Heading back into town, we stopped at the airport to inquire at a couple of small, local airlines. Bush pilots. They'd have no problem dropping us off on the lake. But *we* would have a problem paying for it—$1500 per trip, roughly, at least during the busy time of year. We couldn't afford that—not until I started working and getting paychecks. So we resigned ourselves to giving up, at least temporarily: we'd enjoy the rest of our day and fly back to Anchorage the following day. And we *did* enjoy the rest of our time, meeting some very lovely and friendly people and completely falling in love with the area (with everything except the mosquitoes, as it were). We stopped at one business to ask a question and were immediately invited out back to the owner's house—they couldn't wait to show us their smokehouse (and explain its brilliant design) and share some very recently smoked salmon. We hadn't been in Alaska long enough to cope with that kind of hospitality. It was unbelievable. And the smoked salmon? Meaty. Sweet Smoky. Yet still moist and tender. We've never had better.

Camping on our land would have to wait for another summer.

We decided instead to spend the rest of our summer in the village where I would be teaching. That itself was a valuable and life-changing experience—but a story for another time.

After I'd taught for the two years, I looked for jobs, but none were available in the area near the land. I applied elsewhere, and we spent the next year in Southeast Alaska (another valuable and life-changing experience, but for different reasons). The following spring found us in the Anchorage area again, as we needed to be there to give birth to our first child (the town we'd been living in did not have sufficient facilities for baby delivery—it is common for people who live in villages to travel to Anchorage well ahead of time and wait for the baby to arrive). I went to the annual job fair for teachers and even interviewed with the district I'd been hoping to work for since day one—but they passed on me. I ended up getting a job with the Kenai Peninsula Borough School District, and I have been with them ever since.

After building our home on the Kenai Peninsula (and having another child), it finally became apparent that we were never going to be moving out to that land that had first brought us to Alaska. So roughly ten years after clicking the "place bid" button, I finally sold the land. It was bittersweet—all of those dreams and plans went with it. The imagined hunting trips, mountain traverses, secret berry patches. The millions of acres of wilderness that lay behind (yes, millions). But the dreams and plans had been replaced with others in the meantime—much more *practical* dreams and plans. We're still dreaming and still planning, and I like the fact that we don't have to play the waiting game before putting our plans into action. Maybe one day we'll find ourselves motivated to move a little farther out. There will probably still be land for sale in that same area. But it won't be the same. Alaska won't be new. We won't be as young and naïve. Yet we'd be more likely to make it work.

Our plans have changed so many times since moving to Alaska that I have lost count, but it reiterates an important point: one must be flexible. Things are never going to turn out exactly the way you think they will.

They might end up being a whole lot better.

Land for your needs

As people shop for the perfect parcel (or parcels), they often buy too much land—or the wrong type. Unless you have road access and heavy machinery (such as an excavator or bulldozer), it is of little use to buy any lot with more than one or two acres of high ground (non-muskeg). Some people want 40 or even 100 acres, thinking they will turn it into a productive agricultural homestead with their bare hands.

This is not going to happen.

Land in Alaska is notoriously difficult to clear and work with, and just about the only people who use more than one or two acres are commercial farmers. Most arable land in Alaska is either forested or was previously forested. That means stumps. Removing stumps by hand is hard work (take my word for it). Building quality soil is also a very slow process. To turn 40 acres into a farm using nothing but hand tools would take decades.

Having some extra acreage as forest is not a bad idea—a well-tended forest is a great source of firewood, a source of other useful plants, and habitat for many desirable creatures such as moose, snowshoe hare, hamsquatch, and black bear. But if there is nearby public land (i.e. state-owned) that is wooded, one can usually get a permit for cutting firewood—and there will still be animals to hunt and plants to gather.

Others want the extra acreage as a buffer between them and the rest of humanity. That sounds nice to those sitting in a city or suburb as they read this. But when you actually get out here, you'll find that it's not so much of an issue. Very few people live year-round off grid anywhere in Alaska, and those that do will often only try it for a year or two. You'll find that you actually *want* neighbors nearby in case of emergency (and cabin fever *can* become an emergency). Usually, any neighbors will be there for most of the same reasons—including the desire for space, peace, and quiet. You'll find they want to intrude on you just as much as you want to intrude on them. Besides, Alaska already has a buffer between us and the rest of humanity: Canada.

In other words, don't pay extra for a big lot if you aren't going to use all of it. Save your money. You'll need it for other things. And if you have a big lot, don't clear more of it than you'll actually use. Save your energy. You'll need it for other things.

Buying

I'm not a real estate agent. I have little advice on the actual act of buying land. Buy I did come across a difficulty when buying a parcel this past summer: banks don't really want to loan money for people buying raw land. Giving a home mortgage, to them, is a safer bet: they then have a house with a discernable value as collateral. When it comes to raw land, a lien might not mean anything to the bank, especially if nobody wants to buy the lot in case of default. I've seen people attempt to homestead off-grid and they end up leaving nothing but a terrible mess behind (and a poorly built shack as a residence). The land ends up being a liability rather than an asset. If you have an existing house you can sell in order to finance your adventure, then you should be able to pay cash for your land. If not, some kind of financing will be necessary.

Buying land directly from the state is one option. The state will finance the sale for you. But these lots are often remote and soggy, so due diligence is *essential* for those pursuing this option. If you can't visit it yourself, find an Alaskan you can trust to walk it for you and give some feedback. Even if you have to pay someone for a little bit of their time, it beats wasting your life savings on something that you can't use. I've actually done this for someone using a video call app—it's the next best thing to being here.

A lot of off-grid land for sale by a private party will offer owner/seller financing. This can be a good option. It can also be a terrible option. Some contracts are very honest, straightforward, and don't even charge interest. Some have interest rates that balloon after a certain amount of time (for example, once the buyers are guaranteed to qualify for a permanent fund dividend, also known as a PFD). Some are very overpriced but attractive because of a low down payment.

As of 2019, this price guide should give readers a ballpark idea of what a fair price (in U.S. dollars) is for off-grid land.

- Land with no existing access: if it has no trail, road, or waterfront, you should be paying less than $1,000 per acre (and *much* less if it's a big parcel or mostly muskeg).
- Land with trail or waterfront access only: $1,000 to $1,500 per acre; waterfront on certain rivers or lakes might be more, depending on how desirable the area is.
- Land with road access: $2,000 to $5,000 per acre; again, the variation depends on how much is muskeg vs. forest, what the views are like, if the road is maintained, and so on. If it is very remote (i.e. more than 50 miles from the nearest sizable town), you should find lots for less than $2,000 per acre. If it is in or near a very desirable/upscale area (i.e. Homer, Girdwood, Talkeetna), it can also be very pricey. These lots are also likely to have some improvements such as driveways, cleared areas, and even water wells (the more improvements, the higher the price).

Note that all of these prices are for off-grid land. Land with available electricity (which usually also means maintained roads) will often be more—but you can find some great deals if you look diligently.

Ideally, you should walk the entire property before buying. Talk to local residents and ask lots of questions. Like I said before, you don't want to spend years of savings on land that doesn't suit your needs.

Happy hunting!

Chapter Two: Tools and Building

Author's note: if you are buying an existing home or cabin, this chapter may not be very useful—but if you have plans of building additions or remodeling, you may still want to read it.

Log cabin. Deep snow. Cozy fire inside. Tasty beverage. *Let it snow*, you say. *We've got nowhere to go. We can stay inside here for a week if we want.* Well, maybe—assuming you have indoor plumbing. Otherwise you'll have to dash out to the outhouse every now and then. But that's okay. Outhouses are *so* Alaskan. You'll even enjoy those dashes down the little snowy path to the cute cubicle with the crescent cut out of the door.

But it stops being cute when your butt freezes to the seat (yes, this actually happens). And then you yell for someone to come and help you get unstuck. But they can't hear because the snow dampens all the sound. Eventually they come looking for you and your legs are numb. The rest of you is shivering because of the cold air is rushing in through that adorable little crescent you sawed into the door. What do you even *do* for a butt frozen to a toilet seat?

There are actually several options. You can send someone inside to heat up some water, then drizzle it around the toilet seat repeatedly, letting it venture farther beneath your legs each time. You can use friction—rub vigorously where the skin meets the seat until it slowly separates. Breathing hot air directly on the region is also helpful—if you can get someone willing to stick their head that close to the toilet hole. Whatever you do, don't just pull hard. You don't want to leave your skin and hair stuck to the seat. You need it on your legs.

Planning a home (and outbuildings) in Alaska can be challenging. You have to think about things you'd never have to think about most other places (like making sure a bear can find its way out if it happens to find its way in). Many people want the lodge-like self-contained log house—and why not? They are beautiful. They have a nice feel when you are inside. But log cabins are actually some of the least practical homes you can find (not always, but often). Log cabins were originally popular due to the lack of other materials for building (and the technology of the time, in many cases, as a lack of saw mills meant no milled boards with which to build)—any old miner with an axe could put up a basic log cabin, crack the chinks with mud, and deal with the cold by having a fire constantly burning. With few exceptions, they are usually drafty and require constant heating and regular rechinking (chinking is the act of putting material in the small spaces between adjacent logs). They can be a maintenance nightmare.

I'm sorry to burst your bubble. You probably wanted one of those cabins. You probably saw the Dick Proenneke documentary and said, "That's amazing! I want to do that." It's okay. I said that, too. And you still might build a log house some day. But chances are you'll probably settle for a standard stick frame home—they cost a lot less to heat and take a lot less time (and money, usually) to make. Your home will probably be a lot smaller than you thought. That's actually good, because heating big homes requires a lot of firewood—wood that you will have to be cutting, transporting, stacking, and splitting. It may sound like good exercise. It has a romantic appeal: chopping wood in Alaska. But after a couple of years, the cute wears off the same way the cute wore off of your outhouse.

Designing Your Home

When people start to think about a floor plan to their dream house, they might make a list of rooms they need (or want), make some very basic shapes on a page as to where they should be in relation to one another, draw some arrows that represent the flow of foot traffic, and so on. We think about window placement and natural light. We think about the *feel* of a house.

When designing for Alaska, these ideas are put on the back burner; we design with one very clear priority: heat. How will we keep from losing it? How do we get any extra from the sun that we can? Where we will put our heat source (often a single woodstove) for even heating? How thick are our walls? How thick is our ceiling insulation?

Stove placement and draw

The woodstove is the heart of the year-round Alaska home; it's not so important in homes only kept as seasonal summer residences. In fact, smart design keeps my own home from needing heat from May thru September, while many Alaskans (even my nearby neighbors) have to heat their homes year-round. The woodstove should be on the ground floor (some will put one in the basement if it's actually possible to have a basement—see the upcoming section on foundations), since heat rises. It should be close to the middle; if it has to be more on one side or the other, it should be closer to the north side (which will be colder in winter months).

Many stoves will have an air intake that links to the outside somewhere—these are excellent and will help your stove draw better. If you have a homemade barrel stove (a popular choice due to being lightweight and cheap) or something without an exterior air intake, you'll want a window nearby that can be opened to draw air *in*. This can be really helpful in getting your stove started, especially when atmospheric pressure is making it difficult. You'll also want to make sure your stovepipe is high enough above the roofline for it to draw well (to *draw* means to get the smoke up the pipe and out of the house).

Tip: When installing stovepipe, it will be necessary for it to either go through a wall or go through the ceiling. Make sure to not only use insulated metalbestos pipe for these portions, but also make sure that you don't have two sections of pipe joining together *inside* of a wall cavity. If your stovepipe will be going through the second floor (if you have a second floor), make sure not to plan anything within a couple of feet of it—it can get quite hot and is a burn hazard.

These are woodstove considerations for the design portion of your project—more on woodstoves to come in the "Heat" chapter.

The Arctic Entry

Space is cold. Colder than Alaska. It also lacks oxygen. So when sci-fi writers and space station designers design their space homes, they plan for an airlock: a room between the main chamber and the outside, a place where, once both ends are sealed, oxygen levels can be adjusted. Once oxygen levels are optimal, an astronaut can remove their suit and continue into the main chamber.

Think of your Arctic entry (a.k.a mud room) as an airlock. First of all, it makes everything seem more awesome—like you're living on a different planet (and winter in Alaska can sometimes feel like a different planet, especially when you have to suit up for the really cold temperatures). But it serves a similar purpose: it is a boundary between hospitable temperatures and inhospitable temperatures. It is also a great place to store your boots, coats, snowshoes, guns, and even food. Ideally, every single one of your exterior doors should have a small entryway attached to it as a buffer.

My arctic entry usually stays between 30 and 40 degrees Fahrenheit during winter; this is accomplished by being less insulated than the rest of the house (2x4 wall studs instead of 2x6, 2x6 rafters instead of 2x12, and no insulation in the floor). This is ideal in many ways. First of all, it gives me a place to store food (and to keep my refrigerator so that it hardly ever turns on, saving a tremendous amount of energy). When I open the door to go outside, I'm not greeted with a blast of cold air—depending on the day, it could be well below zero or in the 20s outside. But being greeted with 35 degree air—and no wind—is a huge improvement. It gives a comfortable place to don cold weather gear without getting sweaty (you don't want to sweat before you get outside, or even once you're outside, ideally). When you come in from the outside, it gives you a comfortable place to take off that same gear—without getting mud or snow inside the house (hence the term "mud room"). Also, if you happen to be hunting in winter, bringing your gun directly into the warm house from the cold outside will cause condensation, which will end up causing a need for more regular gun maintenance. It's better to keep them in the entryway, or at least let them sit in there for a while to warm up slowly before bringing them inside.

As you design your home, make sure to utilize Arctic entries. They don't need to be big—mine is only eight feet by nine feet—but they do need to be there. Well, they don't *need* to be there, but your home will be warmer and cleaner, and your life will be easier with them.

Bathrooms

Your bathroom may or may not actually be a bathroom. It may only be a washroom. It may have a bathtub or a shower or neither. It may or may not feature a toilet. It depends on many factors.

The first factor is your home's location. If you do not have road access, it's unlikely that you will be able to install a septic tank. They tend to be big and difficult to transport. So if your location is fly-in, boat-in, or trail access, you probably won't have standard indoor plumbing. That leaves you with two options: outhouse or composting toilet. One requires that you leave the house when you need to go—there will be times that you won't want to do that. Actually, there is a third option: go in the woods, wherever you feel like it. Like a bear.

Whether your toilet is indoors or not, you'll probably want a place to bathe. This will also depend on a number of factors, mainly: from where do you get your water? If you have a well, do you have a way to power the well pump? If so, you can have indoor plumbing, which will likely also include a water heater and modern baths or showers. If you have a hand pump well, that's a different story. If you catch rainwater or haul water from a lake or stream, that has its own issues. If you don't have a well with a powered pump, you'll need a large water tank of one kind or another (this might be anywhere from 20 to 2000 gallons—again, it depends on your location and your ability to get the tank to it).

For those without modern plumbing, baths and/or showers are still a possibility. Sponge baths are always easy. If you have a bathtub or stock tank, you can fill it with pot after pot of hot water from your stove, just like in the very old days. If your water tank is big enough, you can still pump water out of it, through a water heater, and fill your tub without so much trouble. You can also pump from a tank through a water heater into a shower. I've tried all of these. They all have their advantages and disadvantages—and they all work. When designing your home, consider whether or not you'll be able to have indoor plumbing. If you'll need to fill your tub with pots of water from the stove, you'll want the bathroom to be very near the kitchen.

Regardless of where you put your bathroom, remember one thing: you'll need a window to let the moist air out (this goes for your kitchen area as well). Houses that don't vent their moist air end up getting mold problems, especially due to condensation in the winter. Opening a window might sound like a bad idea when the temperatures are well below zero, but you always need to have some kind of air flow coming through your house—you just want to be able to control it (and make sure to get a hygrometer to measure your indoor humidity—it will let you know when you want to let outside air in, inside air out, or both).

Amputating Frostbitten Limbs

Frostbite is your body's way of conserving its essential parts (like the torso, where most of the organs are) at the expense of extremities (fingers, toes, noses); a person can live without a couple of fingers or toes, but it can't live without a heart, lungs, stomach, and other organs. When the cold is extreme, some people apply this same strategy to their home: they close off rooms that aren't necessary. These are usually the ones farthest from the woodstove (extremities). They are allowed to shut down—to freeze—so that the main trunk of the home can stay at a livable temperature, as there is less space to heat. This might mean sleeping on the couch in the living room instead of a bedroom.

If you choose to incorporate this idea into your design, there are some considerations. First of all, you'll want to close the room(s) off and insulate the doorway (this might just be with foam boards). But you'll also want to plan it so that any rooms that *do* get closed off won't be damaged by freezing. This means nothing with plumbing (obviously), but it also means no rooms that have drywall (sheetrock) as interior sheathing. Not a problem for those of you who decide to go the log cabin route. But if you have drywall and there is moisture in the room (because you've been living in it), and then that moisture freezes in the walls, it will damage the drywall.

The workaround for this situation is using something else for interior sheathing—it could be tongue and groove pine boards, it could be painted plywood, it could even be corrugated tin. Ideally, though, it will never be an issue because your design (and all of that awesome firewood you put up) means you won't need to resort to extra-room-amputation.

Sun and wind

Just like in any other climate, the temperature in your home will be heavily influenced by the sun and the wind. Even on moderately cool days, a fierce wind can really suck the warmth out of a house. However, cold winter days with little wind and clear skies can actually add heat to your home—if the design is right. Consider:

there have been many cold, sunny February days when we've gone out hiking or sledding for several hours. Even though the fire has been dying the entire time, we return to find the house warmer than we left it. What is the secret? Larger windows on the south side of the house, a south side that is designed to take advantage of winter sun (single pitch roof with the tall side facing south), and an attached greenhouse (shed roof on the lower half of the south side). The low angle of the sun means it comes almost straight in through the windows.

It is also important to plan for prevailing winds. In many parts of the state, winds are predictable at different times of year. In this part of Southcentral Alaska, winter winds are predictably from the north while summer winds are predictably from the south. There is some variation, of course, and certain storms can always be exceptions, but those directions hold true most of the time. With this in mind, I designed our house to have a single-pitch roof with the low side to the north. This leaves less surface area at the mercy of north winds. By choosing a home site that is on the south/southwest side of a gentle hill, I'm also using local geography to keep heat loss from winter wind at a minimum (home sites on south-facing slopes are almost always the best possible option). One can also take advantage of local trees: having coniferous trees to the north also provides a wind break.

Does this mean our house is unbearably hot in summer? Not exactly. It does get pretty warm at times—a clear day in the mid 60s (a warm summer day by Alaskan standards) means inside temperatures in the upper 70s. We just open windows when we need to. And we heavily ventilate our greenhouse on sunny days by keeping its door and windows open (otherwise it would be too hot for our plants!). Because of our latitude (winter sun angle) and seasonal winds, the smartest design is to have a taller side of the house (with more windows) facing south and a lower side of the house (with fewer windows) facing north. You will want at least one good window facing north whatever the case—so you'll have a nice, warm place to sit when watching the northern lights.

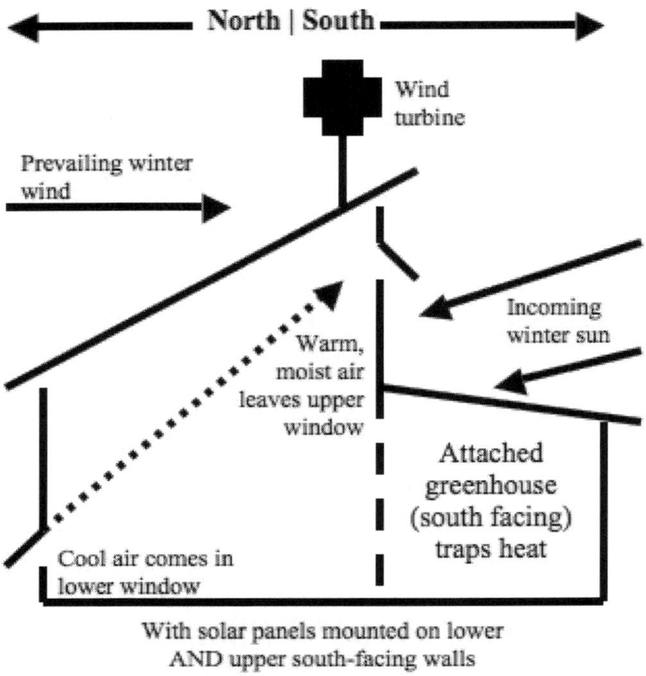

Figure 3: Diagram showing air flow into and out of author's cabin plus winter sun and wind directions

Storage Space and Outbuildings

Many people have rooms in their homes that rarely see use—they might be officially labeled “office,” or “guest bedroom,” or “craft room,” when they are really just storage rooms. In lots of cases, even dining rooms get used only during special occasions. People tend to spend their time in the living room, the bedroom, or the kitchen. Having a lot of rooms in your house that don’t get used for anything other than storage is a waste of interior space—space that must be heated in winter (do I sound like a broken record here?).

If you have equipment that might get used occasionally or seasonally, keep it in a shed when you aren’t using it. Keeping your home just big enough to live comfortably will pay long-term dividends in firewood saved. Some sheds might just be for storage only. I also have a tool shed/work shed (it has a workbench and all), but it’s small and not a comfortable place to work during cold and dark months. We also have a barn/greenhouse building with a lot more space—sometimes I'll build in there if it's raining or snowing. It would be nice to have my own shop, and I just might do that one day—but they are expensive to build, and powering shop tools with an off-grid power system is iffy. I'd have to run a generator anytime I wanted to build something. For now, I'm happy to keep things simple and flexible—portable, battery powered tools to build wherever I need to.

Non-traditional Options

Not every off-grid Alaska home is a standard home or cabin made of rectangles. Some people will drive an old school bus into the woods, put a wood stove in it, and call it a day. Some get small, prefabricated cabins on skids, delivered on the back of a flatbed truck (these are rarely bigger than 12 feet by 20 feet). Some will use a travel trailer or RV (not recommended for winter living, though some will build a house or cabin *around* a parked trailer). Other portable tiny homes are also a possibility, though all of these options depend on road access. Many of these are also good options for places to live while building something bigger.

One popular option that is compatible with more remote locations would be the yurt. There are many people who live in yurts year-round in Alaska. They do have benefits in terms of portability and ease of construction (though they still need a sizable deck to sit on). The downsides are that they are not as quiet (you really hear the wind!) and they do require more heating. Others might opt for a wall tent with a woodstove—many a winter has been spent in these as well, but it's not really a long-term option. Some will live in a wall tent while building a cabin around it—very clever!

Building your Home

After buying your land, analyzing it (for the best possible home site), and designing a home that will be easy to heat in winter and pleasantly warm in summer, you can start making plans to build. Most people plan to start in late spring or early summer so that there is time to finish before things get cold. There should be enough time—unless your home is too large or complex to complete in a few months.

If you have limited time and/or money for building, you might consider a more-on house (pronounced "moron" house): you start with something kind of small, then you add a little more on here, add a little more on there, and eventually it's big enough to be comfortable. You'll just need to have foundation in place ahead of time or have the ability to add more foundation when the time comes. Our house started as a single 12'x26' room—then we added an Arctic entry on the west side, a bedroom on the east side (year one), a sun room and a greenhouse on the south side (year two), then another bedroom and bathroom on the north side (year three). We've run out of ways to add on—but it's enough for our small family.

The following building tips start from the ground up: foundation to the roof.

Foundations

The type of foundation you choose for your home will depend mostly on your local soil and your bank account. If you plan to have anything larger than 12x20 (which can rest comfortably on skids), you'll need something under your house that puts it in contact with soil that doesn't freeze. In many places, that's a minimum of four feet, but it should really go deeper—as deep as possible. The frost line can fluctuate from year to year. If it's a winter without much snow cover, the ground may freeze extra deep due to the lack of insulation above (which it would normally get from snowpack).

If your foundation is not below the frost line, this is what will happen: the soil (and the moisture in it) will freeze. When water turns to ice, it expands. It takes up more space. This causes the ground to rise—it could be a fraction of an inch. It could be several inches (I've personally seen as much as eight, and some people have told me they've seen 18 inches of frost heave). When the soil rises, it doesn't rise the same amount all around. It might come up two inches under your living room but four inches under your arctic entry. This can separate entire rooms from each other. Nails and screws are no match for the power of ice—if ice can split apart a cliff face made of granite, it can break the nails that attach two rooms together. This is why you want your house resting on soil that will not freeze. Plan accordingly.

Basements are actually quite rare in Alaska. To begin with, they are expensive. They also have the tendency to flood in a lot of areas (several businesses do quite well pumping people's basements during wet periods). They can be great when the water table is low and the soil drains well (many parts of Alaska have very slow-draining soils, and continuous rainfall during late summer and fall can saturate soil so thoroughly that ponding occurs on soil that is normally high and dry). If your site is suitable for a basement, there's the obvious storage benefit, and there's also the benefit of tapping into above-freezing temperatures from below the surface—in general, basements stay cool (if unheated) but above freezing. This helps the rest of the house stay warm by providing a cushion of warmer-than-freezing air on one side (the underside) of the living space. Many houses on raised foundations (or cabins on skids) have nothing underneath, so when the temperatures are sub-zero, the living space is being "attacked" on all sides by the cold. If you can eliminate one of those sides, that's a plus.

Possibly the most popular type of foundation for remote and off-grid cabins is the sonotube. The tube itself is like the cardboard tube from a roll of paper towels—but much bigger and stronger. You dig a cylindrical hole into the ground using some kind of earth auger—though a neighbor of mine just used a shovel—and you lower the tube down. Now it serves as a concrete form. What you end up with are concrete "feet" that extend down below the frost line. The advantage of sonotubes is the simplicity. Many a sonotube foundation has been created by a single person working alone. There are disadvantages, though. The concrete itself can crack and disintegrate over time, depending on the pressure from freezing and thawing. In some cases, people have a hard time getting their concrete to set up because water begins to infiltrate the hole they dug for the sonotube (I've seen this fixed by dumping extra cement sacks into the hole to absorb the water…time will tell whether that was a good idea or not, but it's worked well for a couple of years so far). Once again, the deciding factor is the soil (and how water moves through it). If you've checked out the USDA soil report for your area, you should have enough data to help you decide. It's still a good idea to dig a few test holes here and there (4-6 feet deep) and see the soil profile for yourself. It'll also give you a good idea as to how quickly water fills in (if it does at all)—and at these test holes can become outhouses in the future.

Another type of pier foundation that is becoming more and more popular is that of recycled steel pipe. I see it used very often here on the Kenai Peninsula and have used it myself more than once (I have built on it but never installed it—I have a good friend that does the installation). It does require the ability to use heavy machinery (an excavator), which can be costly, but the overall savings make it worthwhile. The pipe itself can be very cheap compared to other foundation options—it is usually bought used in large lots at auction. Once the pipe section (usually at least 15 feet long) is placed upright in position, it is pounded/vibrated down by the excavator (using a vibrator attachment) until it meets enough resistance that it actually begins to lift the excavator off the ground. If needed, multiple sections can be screwed together to go as much as 30 feet or more into the ground—well below the frost line. It is reminiscent of pile driving, but on a smaller scale with a different (hollow) type of pile. Once the upright pieces are in place, they are made the correct height by using a cutting torch to get rid of any extra pipe. Then you can either weld brackets onto the top and link your pipes with wooden beams or you can weld more pipe across the tops horizontally (which is ultimately stronger and longer-lasting than wood).

A third type of pier foundation is the helical pier. These are actually the best type of pier foundation overall, but they are much more expensive than sonotubes or recycled pipe. A pipe with a metal helix at the end (it looks like part of a screw) is rotated—screwed—down into the ground, usually with a portable machine that can get them as deep as necessary. The helix at the end gives it the ability to bear more weight than a metal post of comparable size. Another nice feature is that they come with a sleeve around the pipe—so as the ground freezes, thaws, rises, and falls, the soil moves the sleeve, never the pipe itself. The piers are topped with brackets that can accommodate wooden beams. I know of at least one company (at the time of this writing—Techno Metal Post) that does this, and they go all around the state installing these foundations. Because their pipe driving machine can be driven off-road, they are able to install these foundations in many semi-remote places (trail access is necessary). These are also better for soggy soils (such as certain kinds of muskeg).

A final type of pier foundation is the simplest of all: wood. Treated 4x4, 6x6, or even 8x8 posts are put into the ground, usually in hand-dug holes. Sometimes the bases of the posts are wrapped in plastic sheeting or house wrap to help protect them from water. Then the beams sit atop these posts much like they would sit atop sonotubes or helical metal piers. I've personally used this method for some outbuildings—a goat shed and our barn/greenhouse—but would not recommend it for a dwelling if there are other options available, as this type of foundation will not be as long-lasting as any of the others. Wood, even treated wood, will eventually rot. In some cases, these foundations can be replaced later by one of the other methods, so leave some clearance above ground if you use this method, as you'll one day need to get some pipes or sonotubes under there. Hopefully, if your site is dry, that won't be for a long time.

All of these types of pier foundations are currently in use in my neighborhood. In the past several years, we've had a couple of earthquakes that were 7.0 or greater (on the Richter scale), and none of our local structures have sustained any earthquake damage. That also has a lot do with local soil and geology, but those are actually quite typical for the Cook Inlet lowlands (so you'd find similar conditions in Anchorage and Matanuska-Susitna lowlands as you would here on the western Kenai Peninsula).

I have seen some unfortunate situations in which cheechakos (newcomers) think they can just put their cabin on cement footings that sit atop the ground. This always results in tremendous stress on the structure and eventual failure of one kind or another as the ground shifts unevenly beneath the structure. I have even seen this happen after I've warned people not to try it, yet they try it anyway. While it may be a running theme throughout this book, I'll say it now for the first time: no matter where you go in Alaska, no matter what your situation, talk to the locals—especially those that have been there the longest. Heed their advice. Observe their ways of doing things—there will always be a reason why they do the things they do, and why they do them in a certain way. Some video you saw on the internet probably won't work because it's just not suitable to your local conditions. And locals are usually very happy to help, so don't be afraid.

Floors

I won't bother explaining how to frame a floor (or walls, or a roof)—that is already well-described in other books and better taught by other people. But I will say this: if you do happen to choose a type of foundation that elevates your floor above ground level (i.e. sonotubes, helical piers), I highly recommend that you insulate your floor. Even if you have skirting boards, it will make your house a *lot* easier to heat. It will more than pay for itself in the amount of time and effort you save in cutting firewood.

As for flooring material, options abound—but not all are practical, depending on how remote your location is. Old-time log cabins would have dirt floors, and somehow people survived that way, so take comfort in knowing that you'll have it better (unless you *want* to have a dirt floor, in which case you can take comfort in knowing you won't be the first). Some people don't use any flooring material at all—they just paint their subfloor and call it a day. And it works. Most people in rural Alaska aren't very concerned about keeping up with the Joneses. You don't need shiny hardwood floors. Painted subfloor sweeps well, and you can always cover it with rugs anywhere you want. You can repaint it when it gets scuffed. You can add a layer of plywood after the years have taken their toll. This is the method I used for our Arctic entry.

Other flooring materials:

- Sheet vinyl: nice because you can have a continuous smooth surface that repels water. Good for kitchens or bathrooms. Cleans easily. Non-flammable, so it might be good for areas near your woodstove. The downside is that the rolls are usually 12 feet wide and this can be very unwieldy for people in more remote settings. You also need to install ACX plywood (very expensive) underneath and cement any cracks between sheets and screw indentations (very time consuming). Also requires adhesive and a heavy roller to smooth out the top as you install, though I've seen other methods of attaching it (like staples).
- Plank vinyl/vinyl tiles: come in small boxes, so this solves the portability problem for getting vinyl flooring to remote sites (if you have to fly in or use a 4-wheeler). Installs easily and doesn't need adhesive. If you don't install it well, it might not be as water-repellent (liquids could seep through cracks where the individual tiles meet). Otherwise, this is an ideal flooring material, though it can be pricey.

- Ceramic tile: good for areas around woodstoves as well as the more traditional bathroom applications. It might be a good idea if you like tile, don't mind the work of installing it, and don't have to transport it in a way that is likely to break the tiles (like down a long and bumpy trail or gravel road).
- Hardwood flooring: we put this in a bedroom because I found a great deal on somebody's leftovers. It looks nice, but it requires a special tool for installation (which you'd probably have to rent). It can be pricey, but that's not a big deal for some.
- Rough cut planks: in the old days, people milled basic planks for use as floorboards. We use these in a couple of rooms thanks to having a friend with a mill. They're durable, cheap, and have a nice rustic look. However, they require a lot of sanding if you want them to be smooth, and they'll often have a bit of bend in one direction or the other (depending on the tree they come from). You could just as easily buy 1x6 or 1x8 boards from a building supply store and it would look about the same, but more expensive.
- Carpet: like vinyl rolls, it might be hard to get carpet rolls to certain sites. It's nice and warm, but remember that vacuum cleaners require a lot of power. If you're using solar and/or wind power, you might be limited as to which days you can run a vacuum (we only tend to vacuum our rugs on sunny days when there is excess power). It can be difficult to keep clean if you get moisture issues, and it can also harbor mold.

Walls

There isn't a whole lot that is different about the construction of walls for Alaskan conditions. Here are some pointers.

- Log walls: even seasoned logs will shrink over time. This creates gaps in your walls, between the logs. Walls of a log home will need to be re-chinked several times over the years (unless you enjoy having the wind blow through your house). Most people buy a log-home specific chinking from the building supply store. It goes on with a caulking gun. You can also use various local, natural materials for chinking. You can even use mud (people certainly used to). There are a lot of ways to plug up a hole.

- Stick frame walls: the only thing to remember about stick frame walls is that you need to put vapor barrier (plastic sheeting/polyethylene) on the inside of your studs, between the insulation and your interior sheathing. If you don't, then moisture (have I mentioned that there will be a lot of water vapor inside the house during winter?) that is moving out of the house will freeze along the backside of you *exterior* sheathing, which will be very cold due to being outside in an Alaskan winter. You don't want a sheet of ice inside your wall. You need to keep the moisture on the warm side of the wall and make sure you have adequate ventilation so that it can get out another way (i.e. gable vents or selectively placed upper windows). Wall studs are usually at least 2x6.
- Remote walls: yes, there is something called a remote wall, and it's ideal—if you can plan for it and afford it. The wall itself has standard insulation, but there are rigid insulation boards added along the exterior of the house, then siding is hung from those rigid foam boards. In these cases, the exterior insulation should be 2/3 of the total while the interior should be 1/3 (i.e. 8 inches of foam board on the outside, 4 inches of insulation on the inside). See the Cold Climate Housing Research Center (part of the University of Alaska, Fairbanks) for more information.

Also remember that if you plan to leave any rooms cold and unoccupied during winter, you'll want to use something other than drywall for your interior sheathing (i.e. tongue and groove boards, painted plywood). Rotten, crumbly drywall is no good and not a lot of fun to replace.

On the exterior, most people will add house wrap or tar paper. What's more, many rural Alaskans don't care to add siding on top of this. Some may consider it trashy, but it makes sense for those that can't afford siding (at least not all at once). It's not too expensive to put new house wrap on a cabin every few years, and the wrap does a pretty good job of keeping the weather out. For those in organized boroughs (the equivalent of a county), having a house classified as "unfinished construction" can also keep property taxes lower. We left our exterior as tar paper for our first winter off-grid and we survived, though we did end up adding siding the following summer.

Windows

Ideally you will want double-pane vinyl windows (or something similar). Wooden windows tend to get mold issues. I'll often see discarded wooden windows at the local dump. Being a natural scavenger, I'll inspect to see if they're worth using on a project, and I often leave them due to mold growth (obvious black spots). Another issue with wood windows is that they have to be very well-sealed on the outside, otherwise they soak up water and transfer it into your walls, so be prepared to regularly repaint any wood-framed windows you choose to use.

You'll need some of your windows to open, especially near areas that tend to harbor moisture (kitchen, bathroom) and especially higher up (if you have a loft or second floor) as a way of getting moisture out of the house (higher up is preferable, since warmer air holds more moisture and heat rises). You'll want another window to be able to open up somewhere near your woodstove as a way of drawing air *in* or equalizing pressure (to help get a fire started). Any window that opens should have a screen. Summertime mosquitoes and midges (no-see-ums) are no joke. They will torture you.

Many people plan on having huge picture windows so that they can look out at the lovely Alaskan scenery. It's nothing to be ashamed of. The scenery will probably be a lot better than what you are used to. But you might want to settle for slightly smaller windows for light and scenery—the average insulation value of a double-paned window is R3, whereas your typical 2x6 walls should be R19 or R21. Window placement should be planned carefully and only after you have spent some time at your building site. There should probably be more windows on the south side than the north side, especially for maintaining light and warmth during winter. In summer, the angle of the sun is such that you won't really get direct sunlight through south-facing windows, so there won't be danger of overheating. With planning, you can achieve the perfect balance of light, airflow, and warmth.

Roofs

Most of a home's heat is lost through the roof. It is essential to make sure that your roof is well-insulated or that you have an insulated ceiling below an attic space (in addition to your insulated roof). Either way, your total insulation should add up to about 10 inches, whether that be in a roof that uses 2x12 rafters or 2x6/2x8 rafters combined with an insulated 2x6 ceiling below an attic space—a total insulation value of R38 or greater. Like in your walls, you'll need vapor barrier between the insulation and the interior sheathing.

Like most roofs, you'll need roofing felt on top, ice and water shield in certain areas (i.e. valleys), and some kind of flashing around the edge—standard roofing practices apply. The main difference you find in Alaska is that almost everyone has metal (galvalume) roofing. It is more expensive than shingles, but it's easy to install and it doesn't blow away so easily. Did you know that we sometimes get nasty storms? And unlike other places, it might not be possible to clean up very easily after a big one. It might be too cold or dark or icy. You might end up with an uncovered roof for weeks if you're particularly unlucky.

Metal roofs are also less likely to burn—this is a real issue for many. We do get wildfires in Alaska—huge ones. They just don't get a lot of press because most of them aren't near population centers. But guess where your off-grid paradise is going to be? Probably not near population centers. And house fires will often start on a roof as well, a result of sparks or embers coming from the stovepipe.

Another benefit of galvalume roofing is that it's the safest for rainwater harvesting. If you live somewhere remote, this might be the easiest way for you to get your water.

Tools

Tools are a touchy subject. People have deep opinions about certain ones. They have brand loyalty. I've never had the luxury of being picky about tools—I tend to buy whatever second-hand tools look like they're in good shape. What's more important to me is having the best tool for the job, and (in my situation) the best *power* tools for any job tend to be those I don't have to plug in. This means I use 18 volt battery-powered tools (I keep the batteries charged using our solar/wind power). My wife, who does most of the landscaping and tree-felling/woodcutting, tends to use gas powered tools. Neither require a generator to run, which is important to us.

Running power tools using a generator is not necessarily a bad thing. That makes it possible to use an air compressor (and things like nail guns). If you plan to do a *lot* of building, that might be worth the investment. But if you only plan on building one house and the occasional outbuilding, you might be better off saving your money and keeping it old school—hammering your nails the traditional way. In fact, before I invested in an 18 volt circular saw, I built a couple of small rooms using a handsaw as my *only* saw—and that includes cutting full-sized sheets of plywood. It was tiring and time-consuming, but it got the job done.

To give you an idea of what tools you might need, I'll just go through a list of what gets used the most on our homestead. There might be tools you thought you'd need that you might not actually need—great! Save some money. On the other hand, it's better to have an obscure tool handy just in case.

- Drill: I use an 18 volt drill as both a drill and a driver. It takes all kinds of driver bits, drill bits, and wood auger bits. It's a bit heavy with all of that battery, but you do want awesome triceps, right?
- Circular saw: it can take the place of a chop saw, table saw, and more. Get to know its features (angled cuts, variable blade depth) to get the most versatility. Again, great for the triceps.
- Crosscut saw: for finishing certain cuts where you don't want the circular saw to cut too much. Also a good all-around backup. Can be useful in gardening and magic shows.
- Reciprocating saw: this one is good for cutting holes in things. Also good to have something that can cut through metal. Keep a variety of blades for cutting different materials.
- Tin snips: speaking of cutting through metal, I use these to cut roofing metal, flashing, single-walled stove pipe, and more. Not good for opening tin cans, though.
- Hammer: for basic framing and thumb-bashing. Silver hammers are too fancy for hitting normal things and are

better reserved for skulls, apparently. Just use a regular one for construction.

- Measuring tape/square/level: because it's good to be accurate. And it's hip to be square. Huey Lewis is right, as usual.
- Sledgehammer: for breaking things and driving fence posts. Do not try using Peter Gabriel as a sledgehammer. I tried this once and he just complained. When he says he wants to be one, he only means it figuratively. My mistake.
- Hedgeslammer: for slamming hedges.
- Posthole digger: I use the auger style for deep holes about six inches in diameter. These can be for post foundations (I use them on outbuildings) or fence posts. Also good for digging shallow wells if you get an extension. I can't think of any pop music reference that goes with posthole digging.
- Digging bar: this is a HEAVY metal bar with a flat blade on one end. It can break through a lot of things (like tree roots) and can provide tremendous leverage when needed. These are more useful than heavy metal bars, where bearded people sit around drinking lager, playing air guitar versions of Megadeth songs, and telling the story of the first time they saw Iron Maiden.
- Ladders: at a minimum you'll want a regular 6 foot ladder and a good extension ladder. More ladders would be better.
- Mallet: sometimes pieces of wood need a bit of encouragement to fit where they need to go. You want to encourage them without destroying them. Rubber mallet.
- Wood chisels: these are handy for fine work (notching) and for hanging doors.
- Clamps: because sometimes you need an extra hand or two.
- Utility knife: just make sure you retract the blade after using.
- Random hand tools: screwdrivers, scissors, wrenches, ratchet set, and so on.
- Pry bar: great for wedging things apart, pulling nails, and wielding maniacally.
- Chains: we use chains for hoisting things, dragging things (i.e. pulling logs), getting neighbors' cars out of ditches, and the occasional freaky Saturday night. Of pulling stumps.

- In the garden:
- Shovel: for digging in the dirt and spoon-feeding the brown bears.
- Clippers/shears: for pruning trees/shrubs and getting rid of saplings.
- Trowel: I don't need to tell you how to use a trowel.
- Mattock: great all-around digging and destruction tool. Also provides excellent leverage.
- Weed whacker: we have a gas powered and a manual (also called a "D-ring"). Great for getting rid of grass and weeds. Not a lot of Alaska has nice, level soil. Unless a bulldozer has been over it, it probably isn't lawnmower compatible.
- Chainsaw: for felling trees and bucking firewood.
- Axe: for felling trees when you want to feel more like Abe Lincoln. Also good for splitting firewood (though you'll probably want a specific splitting maul for that).
- Hatchet: for small axing. Or regular axing for very small people.

Does that seem like a lot? It kind of is. And there are actually a lot more tools that can be useful in these situations, but we're trying to be *practical* here. If you're going to be remote or semi-remote, you'll have to plan carefully and start with only the tools you absolutely need—since you'll have to haul everything in. If you have road access, there shouldn't be any problems (other than cost).

Things *not* to build

This section only exists because I've compiled a running list of things I've seen people build that end up being abandoned or useless. If you don't want your property littered with structures left to rot, pay heed (actually, everything will rot eventually—it seems to happen a lot faster up here thanks to the freeze/thaw cycles, the moisture, and the heavy wear).

One that might not be so obvious is a fence. You might think it silly to put up a fence in the middle of nowhere, but there are plenty of silly people in the world that think it would be a good idea. Some fences are not so bad—like those that keep your chickens or goats in when you need them in. But building fences to keep things *out* will simply not work. I had neighbors that built a giant fence (out of pallets) that stretched for hundreds of feet. They were afraid of bears. But any interested bear would just walk around the fence. Or knock it over. Building fences to keep things out will only work if it is at least 10 feet tall and has no openings except for a strong, reinforced gate. That's a lot of fence. More than anyone would care to haul out into the woods.

I have fences around my apples trees. One day this past summer, I walked out to look at them and found that one of my fences had been pushed down by a curious moose. Normally that would mean the end of the apple trees. But in my case the trees were all perfectly fine. I'm fully aware that no fence would stop a motivated moose. So I strategize: I keep my apples trees in several small orchards with anywhere from 3-7 trees in each one. That way if a moose gets into one orchard, it's not the end of the apple crop. More importantly, I tidy the area on the inside of the fence. This means that there isn't anything inside the fenced area that a moose would want to eat (apart from apple trees, but those are not a moose's normal fare). I also make sure that there is abundant moose browse (i.e. young birch trees, willows, etc.) everywhere else so that moose have no reason to get curious about my apple trees. Apart from a few cleared areas, I keep the property in its natural state. And I also let the local plants do their thing in the places between my cleared areas (cleared areas being backyard, garden beds, orchards, chicken coop, etc.). Not only is it good moose browse, it also maintains healthy soil.

Another superfluous structure I've seen is an outdoor kitchen. It may seem like something nice to have in suburbia—a place where you can do food prep for barbeques and cook the side dishes in the same place at the same time. How novel! But in bear country, it spells bear visits. Which can be good, if you're trying to attract bears. Some people do. The people who built an outdoor kitchen really didn't want bears around, yet they cooked outdoors and also stored a lot of food (and their trash) outdoors. The only time I've seen bears in the neighborhood was during the period of time that they were neighbors—otherwise bear sign is rare, even though the river is very near. The bears know where the good food is: it's in the river valley. Or it's on the muskeg. For a brief period, it was at a cabin between the two.

Adding on to a house can be done easily. There are a few additions I've seen that are definitely unsafe. These are when someone adds on *vertically*—and then they keep going. This is sometimes done in order to maintain a nice view. I drive by one such house on a regular basis: it resembles a pyramid, each floor with an a-frame shape, each floor smaller than the one below it, each floor adding more weight to a bottom floor that was only designed to hold a standard Alaskan snow load. When your house gets 40 or 50 feet tall, just quit. Forget about the view. It is going to collapse. Just hope your aren't inside when it happens.

Step-by-step: Our Attached Greenhouse/Sun room

What follows is a brief explanation (with pictures) of the construction of the attached greenhouse and sun room on the south-facing side of our home. You'll see the first photo is nothing but the pipe foundation.

Figure 4: Halfway ugly wall and metal pipe awaiting an addition

Note that there is a 2x6 bolted (with nails and lag screws) to the house at both the bottom and the top of the space. You'll also notice ugly, flappy tar paper. That's okay. The wind makes it flappy. The tar paper will not be there forever.

Figure 5: The addition taking shape with floor joists, walls, subfloor, and most rafters

Both the floor joists and the rafters (2x6s) have been hung from metal joist hangers (and also nailed, 2 nails on each side). Plywood (3/4 inch tongue and groove) has been added as subfloor. For the greenhouse section, the wall will be a modified post-and-beam style, whereas the sunroom is standard stick-frame construction with studs spaced at 24 inches. There are still several rafters left to be added.

Figure 6: Now with sheathing! Solar panels have been moved, siding has been added, and the greenhouse is almost ready for upper windows.

Sheathing has been added to the sunroom and the exterior sheathing now sports tar paper, windows, and solar panels. A bay window enclosure has been added around the upper (loft) window—this is to add an extra mini-greenhouse area but also to keep snow accumulation on the roof of the sunroom from leaking into the walls of the main cabin. Diagonal braces have been added to the greenhouse walls. The roofing material has been added to both rooms—galvalume for the sun room and corrugated plastic for the greenhouse. Plexiglass leans against the building, waiting to be framed and installed as the main greenhouse windows.

Figure 7: Greenhouse and sun room with locally-milled rough spruce plank flooring

Interior sheathing (tongue and groove pine boards) has been added to the sun room, and rough spruce planks (locally milled) have been added above the subfloor. That ugly tar paper is gone! Hooray! All that remains is for the door to be hung and some siding to be added.

Chapter Three: Food

Now that you've built your dream log cabin, take a break. You must be hungry. Have a sandwich.

It's not very well known, but the best food to be found in Alaska is just laying in the ground. Not *on* the ground, but in the ground. You just have to know where to dig. If you're lucky, your local forest might be home to that most delicate of all Alaskan delicacies: the Arctic truffle. Unlike its warm-climate cousin, the Arctic truffle cannot be detected by any domesticated animals—not that we're aware of, anyway. Some have tried training their dogs to sniff truffles, but I haven't heard of any being successful. Again, knowledge of soil types and drainage are your best friend. Arctic truffles grow exclusively near the root system of balsam poplar trees on south-facing slopes—but only in silt loam soils with at least 6 inches of organic mat on top. That might sound rare, but it isn't really—not if you know what you're looking at. You'll find these delectable nodules—about the size of a walnut—growing in small clusters at the bottom of the organic mat. Look for telltale lichens to lead the way.

But if digging for fungus isn't your thing, that's cool—there's a lot of other food to be had out there. I'm going to go ahead and burst your balloon right now, though: you won't be hunting big game (successfully) if you're going to be living on the road system. Here's the thing about living on the road system: no matter how far out you are, it's still an easy drive to *somebody*. Actually, it's still an easy drive to thousands of people, and a lot of them like to hunt. The result is that when moose season comes around, every hunter that lives in the city gets in his pickup and drives to the end of some back road, thinking that surely nobody has thought of hunting here before. At the end of that back road he'll find several other city hunters there who thought the same thing. The end of this back road is probably where you were planning on moving, wasn't it? The best of both worlds? Remote, yet accessible? So be prepared to chain up your driveway during moose season if you live anywhere on the road system, because it's almost guaranteed that some guy from Anchorage will drive on it if you don't.

The same goes for fishing—if you're on the road system, it'll be a struggle. A fight. We use the term "combat fishing" because it can be just that: thousands of people fighting for a spot along the best stretches of river. Even so, you'll probably have more luck fishing than hunting big game, though it really depends on the year.

It's important to get that out of the way early on, because it seems like everyone who moves up here thinks they're going to get a moose every year and a whole bunch of salmon, and it just isn't like that. It might have been like that many years ago. Most of us buy most of our food at the grocery store. Those that live off the road system might get more wild food, but mail-order groceries still make up the bulk of what is eaten in the bush. I don't need to tell you how to shop at a grocery store. But I do have some ideas on how to spend as little time and money at the grocery store as possible.

Wild plants

There are endless wild edibles in Alaska—if you know what to look for. *And* if you're willing to accept new tastes. Not all of these plants will taste like the plants you are used to. Many of the greens will seem bitter, but they're still very good. You'll want to buy a guide to wild edibles—one with excellent photographs and vivid descriptions. I recommend the one by Janice Schofield Eaton—there's a full-length version, though we've only ever used the pocket version (and the cover says "Janice J. Schofield," in case that helps you find it). I'll cover the basics of wild plant foods here, and by season. It would be a good idea to have a wild plant guide handy, as I'm not going to include pictures of every single plant mentioned.

Spring: The first spring food is actually liquid. Before you see leaves on anything, the sap will begin running in birch trees (alder trees as well, but they're utilized less often). You can tap birch trees for their sap and either drink the sap as it is or make it into syrup. It tastes like lightly sweet, extra-refreshing water—and it *is* mostly water, but it has some sugar and vitamin C and other good nutrition (to tap trees, simply drill a 3/8 inch hole about an inch deep at a slightly upward angle—so the sap will drip down out of the tree—and stuff a bit of plastic tubing in there. Attach a container to the tree and put the tube so it drips into the container. Use only healthy, mature trees, and let them heal after you've tapped them.). Soon, plants will start to leaf out. The first leaves on willows are edible and prized by people in rural parts of the state (places where buying lettuce at the grocery store is prohibitively expensive). They are a traditional food for many and a cause for celebration: they mark the arrival of spring. They're also prized by moose, so don't try to compete with them if they're hanging around. Moose are a lot bigger than you are. I hope. There is a lot of other spring growth that is edible, but only for a limited time—such as fireweed, horsetail, and ferns. The topmost new leaves on fireweed are great, but they get more and more bitter as time goes on. Ferns are edible when still in "fiddlehead" form, and quite delicious—just make sure you don't eat them after they start opening up. They can give you quite a stomach ache. Horsetail is more often used as a medicinal plant, but it is also food in the earlier part of spring. Some of spring's first flowers are also great, such as dandelions and geraniums. Of course, dandelion greens are also fantastic—it's a useful plant all around. There are numerous other wild greens; see them in your guide (I'm only mentioning the most common and abundant ones). The new growth at the end of spruce branches (spruce tips) are also good to munch on—they're also good for making tea and brewing beer (in place of hops).

Summer: The berries come out in summer and are the main focus of anyone who gathers wild plants. The first to come are cloudberries, known in some areas as "salmonberries." They look like raspberries (in terms of shape), but grow on small stems in muskeg areas. They are a light orange color reminiscent of apricots and they have a delicious flavor—very sweet and unique. Next up are blueberries. Most blueberries picked in the Pacific Coast area (i.e. Southeast Alaska, Prince William Sound, the southern coast of the Kenai Peninsula around to the south shore of Kachemak Bay) are the highbush variety. These can grow larger and in great abundance and you'll be in berry heaven when you find a good patch. Huckleberries (closely related red versions of blueberries, basically) grow in these same areas—most berry pickers focus on areas of new growth after a place has been logged. Blueberries most everywhere else in Alaska tend to be bog blueberries that grow on muskeg. They are smaller and tend to be a lighter shade of blue. The nice thing about finding a good patch of muskeg for berries is that it will usually feature several kinds of berries, and you can keep visiting the same patch for months and get different kinds of berries. Next up will be crowberries (known as blackberries in some areas). They are very very very very very dark blue and grow in small bunches on small stems that resemble spruce branches. They have a nice flavor but a large seed—most people don't bother with them, but we like to pick them at the same time as blueberries and just put them in the same container as a way of "extending" the blueberries. They go nicely together. The berries themselves also last longer into fall because of their tougher skin, and they only get better as the year goes on. Other summer berries that are less abundant are watermelon berries, serviceberries, wild strawberries and raspberries, highbush cranberries, currants, and nagoonberries (if you're lucky enough to find some). All of these other less-abundant berries tend to grow on higher ground (not so much on muskeg or tundra)—they're nice snacking, but it's hard to find patches big enough to pick extra to save for winter. There are also poisonous berries—baneberries are the main type. To me, they're easy to identify, as they have a feature that the edible berries don't have: a valley going from the top of the berry to the bottom. A crack, if you will, much like you'd see on a peach. Because of this crack, I think of them as "buttberries." Nobody wants to eat buttberries. They're usually red or white (don't eat any white berries in general).

Fall: There should still be blueberries and crowberries in the beginning of fall. As you continue to pick these, you'll notice lingonberries (also called lowbush cranberries) growing in bunches. They will be on the same muskeg as the other berries, but you'll also find them on high ground, growing around the base of mature trees. They are dark red and tangy, but very good. They should be picked after a good, hard frost. Another great wild food that should be picked after a good frost is the rose hip. They grow on wild rose bushes and look red and plump—kind of like miniature apples (they are related). Some people make pies or jams out of rose hips. You can eat them raw, if you'd like. We like to dry ours and save them for making tea in the winter. They are a tremendous source of vitamin C—most commercial vitamin C supplements actually use rose hips as the main source of the ascorbic acid. All of these other berries have tremendous health benefits—not just vitamins, but also antioxidants, phytonutrients, and so on.

Winter: Plants stop growing in winter. Most of us just eat the berries and greens we saved from the time of year when they were growing, but you can still find some food if you know where to look. The main winter wild plants you'll find are still lingonberries—some people pick them all winter if they know where to find a patch that isn't covered in snow. The other wild plant food sometimes exploited in winter would be cambium. This is the layer beneath the bark of certain trees (birch, in particular) and it is technically edible—but it is usually only eaten in times of starvation. I've never been starving so I haven't tried it. I'll try it soon just for kicks and put the information in the next edition of this book. Otherwise, enjoy your frozen greens and berries and jams. You worked hard for it.

Wild animals

I've already complained about how difficult it is to hunt big game in the more populated parts of the state (and I will again before this chapter is over). But that doesn't mean you can't supplement your diet with good, local, wild meat.

Moose can still be on the menu. But not for the squeamish: most people I know that have moose in the freezer have it there because the moose was a road kill. Many parts of Alaska have an official system for dealing with road kill moose. People interested in the meat sign up for the road kill list. When a moose collision occurs, the state troopers (or local police) call the next person on the list (though it does depend on the area where the collision occurs). It is then that person's duty to get to the scene promptly (even if it's the middle of the night) and haul the moose carcass away. The quality of the meat will be unpredictable. It can be a big old tough moose. It can be young and tender. It can be mostly demolished from the collision or it can be mostly intact. Regardless of its condition, the person called to come get it has to take it away. Even places that don't have an official road kill list will still find ways to salvage any road kill moose they're aware of—it's just more likely to be neighbors working together to get it off the road and divide it up. Road kill moose also often go to tribal elders or local charities (like senior centers).

The road kill list also comes in handy when moose get poached. Depending on the situation, an illegally hunted moose might go to the next person on the list (though the troopers will probably keep at least part of the head as evidence).

In terms of other kinds of big game, the most practical to hunt for food is black bear. Caribou are great if you live in an area with a herd—but those tend to be in more remote areas (if they aren't, though, then go for it—caribou is delicious and my favorite of wild Alaskan meats). Dall sheep and mountain goats are almost always in very remote areas and require either heavy hiking or a helicopter to get near—for serious hunters only (and those with lots of time and/or money to spend). Sitka blacktail deer are a nice size and easy to hunt, but they only live in a few areas: Kodiak Island, Prince William Sound, and Southeast Alaska. There are elk on a couple of islands as well. But black bears can be found most anywhere in Alaska (except for the farthest northern and western reaches) and are usually quite tasty. Furthermore, most hunting units don't have a size or gender requirement on black bears, so you don't have to worry about identifying it before you shoot (only to the extent that you know it's a black bear). Some areas allow bear baiting, which makes it a lot easier (though it adds an ethical dilemma for many). Brown bears are not usually eaten. You have to be desperate for meat to do that.

Small game varies depending on location. The most abundant is often snowshoe hare: they become numerous on a ten-year cycle. If it happens to be the high point in the hare cycle, you'll see them everywhere. When the population crashes, you won't see any. But they'll be back. I've hunted dozens of hares in a single winter and we found that you can do just about anything with the meat—it is versatile. The skins also make nice hats and mittens if you're willing to tan and sew them. Other small game that can be tasty (if you're willing to try it) are squirrels and porcupines. Squirrels don't give much meat, and porcupines are hard to process, but both will feed you if you are hungry.

Then there are birds. The most abundant birds tend to be grouse (spruce grouse, usually) and ptarmigan (willow grouse). These birds tend to be very easy to shoot and taste a lot like chicken (though you might not want spruce grouse once it gets to be midwinter or later—they start tasting pretty sprucey). Waterfowl are abundant in certain seasons and require federal permits for hunting, but they are bigger and tastier than the local birds. People in bush areas tend to hunt them more often, and they will make use of a variety of ducks, geese, swans, and cranes. Note that an Alaska hunting license is insufficient for hunting migratory waterfowl—you also need a federal permit (since they don't *just* live in Alaska—they live in other states as well, and even in other countries). Fear not, a "duck stamp" (as they are called) is easy to get and is usually available at the local post office.

In times of desperation, people make use of other birds. Songbirds. Ravens. Crows. Seagulls. In some areas, seagull eggs are gathered seasonally. Seagulls themselves may be hunted, but usually younger ones—and they're never hunted anywhere near a dump. Nobody wants to eat a dump seagull.

Anecdote: Poaching the Poachers

Ever since we moved off-grid, there have been poachings in the neighborhood. I'm sure they were going on before we moved here, but we didn't know about them. Every poaching seemed to coincide with a time when hunters were down from Anchorage for moose season. After the second year in a row (with a poached moose found in our neighborhood), the wildlife troopers let us know a little too much, and then everyone knew *exactly* who had been doing the poaching. And we were none too happy about it. The rest of us try to hunt according to the rules. When somebody takes a sublegal bull out of the local population, it makes things harder for the rest of us.

But this story isn't about those particular poachers. They know better than to come around and try that again (or so I'd like to think). What they do have in common with the most recent offender is that they aren't from around here. It seems that people who haven't adapted to the local rhythms tend to get a bit overexcited when they come to the area. They're away from the city. They want to shoot something. Ooh, there are moose here! Let me at them!

The story goes like this: my wife's mother came to visit halfway through our most recent moose season. It was her first night visiting in several years, and we were excited for her to see how much progress we had made. After getting in a little bit later than usual (due to a delayed flight), we had some food. No sooner had we sat down than we heard a couple of 4-wheelers driving on the road that runs by our house—but it was already about 9:30, and too dark for hunting in the middle of September. Only the tiniest hint of light remained. We didn't think anything of it and assumed they were just passing by. Except that 20 minutes later, we heard very loud gunshots from very near the house. I knew right away what had happened. I knew I was going to take a look. And I knew I might potentially be running into poachers that didn't want to get caught. But I also knew that the poaching had to stop.

I grabbed a gun—just in case—and hopped in the Jeep, driving just around the corner to the head of a 4-wheeler trail. From this point, the trail leaves the road and heads south, level for a while as it crosses through grassy brush before dropping down into the river valley, where it is more densely wooded with white spruce. Neighbors were already texting me, asking if the shots were mine. I told them "no." They want to know if I wanted help, so I said to come armed or not at all. Some of them did. And when they met me at the head of the trail, I told them to have someone wait at the other end of the trail—at the place where this 4-wheeler trail came back up out of the river valley to meet our road again, roughly a quarter of a mile away. I already knew the poachers weren't going to be coming my way. If someone waited at the other junction (farther south, still on the same side of the river), the poachers would not be able to get past us—not without crossing the river or taking a very long way around.

I had peeked down the trail with my headlamp. They already knew I was on their trail—they'd heard me driving up and seen the headlights—and had started heading the other direction. Once they were moving that way, I drove down the road to where I knew they'd be coming out—heading them off at the pass, right? Sure enough, my neighbor was waiting for them, standing on the road holding an AR-15 and looking very serious. There were two 4-wheelers on the trail, lights off. They'd been trying to get away secretly. He wasn't letting them pass. I'd had the foresight to bring a camera, so I walked up to the two poachers to get photos. I recognized the first one. I didn't need his photo. But I took a picture of the second one. Even though it was dark, the flash worked beautifully and I got a crystal-clear shot.

We didn't try to detain them any longer. We had the proof we needed—except for a carcass. So after they left, we drove the trails with my neighbor's 4-wheeler for a while, looking for anything obviously disturbed—broken branches, matted grass, vehicle tracks, or maybe a giant trail of blood. But it was so dark that we couldn't see anything. We gave up and went home, hoping we'd be able to sleep once the adrenaline wore off.

A little before 8:00 the following morning, I headed outside with my dogs. They immediately ran cross country, straight to where the moose lay. It was only 250 yards from my house, and only about 100 yards from where the 4-wheeler trail left the road. I walked the road to the trailhead and followed the sound of the dogs. I waded through some tall grass to a place where I could see it was smashed down, and there he was: a young bull, probably only a year and a half old. Nowhere near legal. He was clean and cold, covered in dew—it had been cool overnight, probably between 30 and 40 degrees. But it was going to be hot that day—probably over 60 in another hour or so. That's hot for September in Alaska.

I explained the situation to the wildlife trooper once she returned my call. The window for salvaging the moose before it got too hot was closing quickly. By the time she arrived, several neighbors were already standing around the moose. She'd given us the go ahead to at least let the guts out so it could stay as cool as possible for as long as possible. The gut pile was soon on the ground, extending our window for processing the meat. In situations like this, the moose is supposed to go to a local charity. But by the time someone from a local charity would be able to get way out to my place, it would have been too late. The trooper gathered her evidence (by using a chainsaw to cut into the skull and remove the rack) and consented to let us continue processing the moose. It had technically been left in the field to rot (by the poacher), and the amount of time it had been there might have allowed it to qualify as unsafe for a charity—but not unsafe for those of us already there and ready to take it away. We started by using a 4-wheeler to drag it through the grass until it was on the trail. Then we used an electric winch to get it in the back of a trailer (hooked to a different 4-wheeler) and drove it down to a neighbor's shop, where we hung it and skinned it.

That moose skin is now hanging in our barn, stretching. My wife works on it when she can. Most of the meat is in a neighbor's freezer. We eat more of it than anyone else, though it's still technically community meat. And it's good meat. The investigation ended up being widely publicized. The troopers started by talking to the one poacher I'd recognized: a former student of mine, still a minor. I don't know how they laid it out for him, but he cooperated. Not only did he admit that they (he and his uncle) had poached the moose, he took the troopers to where they had ditched their guns in the woods down in the river valley. He took the troopers to another moose carcass that he and his uncle had poached, and also to a third that he knew about—even though he hadn't been present for it. The trooper used the photograph I'd taken and matched it to its location so it could be used as evidence. Once the uncle was officially charged and court documents were filed, the story was picked up by some of the bigger news outlets in the state.

What was even bigger news came in early December. The poacher had decided to plead guilty and was sentenced to 9 months in prison and fines totaling more than $100,000. This story was picked up by the Associated Press, and I even saw a version on the Washington Post website (and it did mention how a local teacher had recognized one of the poachers, etc…yay for me!). In the meantime, social media had been hard at work. Locals had reached out to known associates of the poacher in order to get more background, as he'd only arrived in Alaska less than a year before. The story got weirder and weirder: the guy was supposedly a lifetime criminal with many charges in his former home county (including many felonies), yet he never seemed to go to jail for very long (and sometimes not at all). Some said he was an FBI informant. Either way, it became clear that he was on probation in this other state and had only been allowed to come to Alaska in order to live with his father. Technically, he was being released into third-party custody. This got a lot of people wondering how often that kind of thing happens. Nobody wants their neighborhood to be a dumping ground for out-of-state criminals.

The thing that bothered me the most about the whole episode was that the moose was shot so close to my home. Not only that, but they were shooting from the trail in the direction of my home. If they hadn't hit the moose, they very well could have hit the house. Even though I hadn't heard anything that sounded like a bullet hitting the wall, I still did a cursory check for bullets. You never know. There might still be one lodged in the siding. They can be small and easy to miss.

We will be having a moose roast tomorrow. There are still plenty of those left in the freezer.

Domesticated plants

One of the best things about Alaska is that the local ecosystems remain intact for almost all of the state—very little land has been cleared for farms, cities, and the things that end up destroying biodiversity in the rest of the world. Because of this, our local plant and animal communities resemble what they've been for thousands of years. This is becoming more and more rare everywhere else, so I hesitate to recommend clearing much area for gardening. But gardening doesn't have to be done in a way that harms your local ecosystem.

In fact, having intact ecosystem in close proximity (and even within) your garden is great for soil health, as the natural mycorrhizal fungi will benefit the things you plant (some people spend a fortune buying the stuff and putting it in their soil, not realizing that it already exists in your soil as long as you don't get rid of it by doing something stupid like bulldozing a big garden area, which still seems to happen all the time because everyone seems to think gardens should be flat and rectangular). With this in mind, we have several small garden areas separated by native vegetation. We build raised beds using logs from a nearby slash pile; the wood itself will end up benefitting the soil over time as it breaks down (and the wood was free).

We build soil health by adding compost from our compost pile, kelp from local beaches (after rinsing it), the sawdust we sweep out of the chicken house (nicely encrusted with chicken manure), the straw we rake out of the goat house (nicely encrusted with goat manure), and so on. When we run low of different kinds of soil amendments, we will sometimes gather moose nuggets on our walks—they're also good for the soil, though you ideally want it as fresh as possible and during the time of year that they're eating greenery (more nitrogen that way). We water our gardens using collected rain in barrels and other containers—ideally later in the day after it has warmed up. Using freshly pumped groundwater can shock your plants due to its cold temperature, so warmed rainwater is the best way to go. If we're lucky, spring and summer rains are frequent enough that we don't really have to water that often.

As for the plants themselves, we focus on the vegetables that grow well outside—peas and carrots (always together), potatoes, beets, radishes, turnips, potatoes, mustard, collard greens, kale, and so on. Spinach always bolts and isn't worth the time (it's because of the sunlight/day length). We do grow some things in a couple of greenhouses—green beans, tomatoes, cucumbers, and peppers—but these are in limited numbers. Greenhouses and high tunnels (also known as "poly tunnels") are very popular in Southcentral Alaska because our summers don't get very warm; the tunnels and greenhouses allow people to grow their vegetables a lot faster and in greater quantity per square foot. People can also grow things that otherwise wouldn't grow well in Alaska. This is all fantastic news for those willing to put in the effort. We don't bother with tunnels, simply because they usually require a ventilation system to keep from getting too hot—and this would require either a lot of battery power (and a thermostat system) or the kind of attention we just don't want to spend on vegetables. We have friends that use a high tunnel very successfully, growing tremendous amounts of vegetables in the summer—but they rarely leave their property, except for on gloomy days when they don't have to worry about their tunnel overheating.

Grains grow well in certain areas—particularly in the Interior. Barley, oats, and wheat are grown mostly near Delta Junction, but there are also some grains grown in the Fairbanks area and near Anderson. Grains have also been grown in the Matanuska/Susitna area, but not as successfully. They're hardly worth mentioning, mostly because they're not very practical to grow on a small scale—not when compared to something like potatoes. Most in the grain farming business have large acreages and all of the modern farming implements, and that's just not within the reach of very many people (not without mortgage-sized loans, anyway). That kind of operation also requires level land, which means it has to be dozed, which also means that much of the most fertile soil (the topsoil) has probably been scraped off and put in piles along with slash and stumps, which means that the soil will need fertilizer on a large scale, and before we know it we're back in Kansas again.

That brings us to fruits, which are my favorite thing to grow. We know that much of Alaska abounds with wild fruit. If you have a good wild berry patch, you may never have to grow any fruit. Unfortunately, the wild berries have good years and bad years. We recently had one of our best years ever for wild berries—2016—but the following year had almost no wild berries in our area. We didn't even bother after a couple of tries. Fortunately, some of my apple trees decided to go crazy that summer. No blueberries, but plenty of apples. Diversifying is a good thing.

Yes, apples can be grown in Alaska. There are a number of varieties that do quite well, and the Alaska Pioneer Fruit Growers Association has gone to the trouble of documenting which types are the best suited for Alaska (and you can find the information on their website). Of course, different types do better in some areas compared to others. Apple growers in the Interior (like the Fairbanks area) are limited to fewer types simply because their winters get so much colder. On the other hand, apple growers in Southcentral Alaska don't get as much light and heat in the summer (compared to the Interior), so their apples might not grow as large.

Other tree fruits that *can* be grown in Alaska are pears, plums, apricots, and cherries. However, these rarely do well and require the hottest of Alaskan summers to ripen. Even though they may be able to survive our winters, they don't thrive in our summers (familiarize yourself with plant hardiness zones—the USDA has maps that show which hardiness zones can be found where—and these will tell you which perennial plants can survive the winter if you look up the plant variety's hardiness rating). Some people just put fruit trees inside of their high tunnels, making it possible to grow a wider variety of fruits (including peaches, kiwis, and more). There is a heated greenhouse at Manley Hot Springs that uses the natural geothermal heat to grow things like grapes—very impressive for a place that can see -70 temperatures in the winter. The decision of what to grow inside of high tunnels and greenhouses tends to divide people in a philosophical way. Some people grow the normal Alaska fruits and vegetables but use the improved conditions to have bigger fruits/vegetables and better yields. We prefer to use our greenhouse to grow things that otherwise wouldn't really grow in our area—things like tomatoes, cucumbers, and peppers. Some people do both.

Anyhow, back to fruit. Domesticated berries do very well in Alaska and are more predictable than the wild berries. Strawberries and raspberries are both mainstays of almost every homestead garden in the state. Another good berry to grow is the honeyberry. They're a Siberian berry that is perfectly adapted to most Alaskan climates. Our honeyberry bushes are usually the first thing to get green in the spring—and also the first things to produce fruit. The berries are similar to blueberries, but slightly more elongated (kind of bell-shaped) and tangy. They produce abundantly—but they're easy food for birds, so you may have to find ways to discourage those birds from feasting on your berries. Currants also do well, as do serviceberries.

Whatever you decide to grow in your garden, there are some guidelines that will serve you well no matter where you live in Alaska:

- Gentle south-facing slopes are the best for growing just about anything. The south-facing land get more heat and light overall; gentle slopes drain well but not so well that you have to water all of the time. You can also create your own south-facing slopes by mounding soil in and east-west direction and planting on the south side of the mounds (look up hugelculture: it is the use of old logs to build dirt mounds for planting. The logs help retain heat and moisture, and they improve soil health as they decompose over the years.).
- Wind is one of the worst enemies of your domesticated plants. This is one reason to use greenhouses and high tunnels. If you can't afford a bunch of greenhouses, think about wind protection before you clear garden areas—you'll want coniferous trees acting as a windbreak between your garden and the prevailing winds (you'll also need to know the local prevailing wind directions for different times of year).
- Moose are the other worst enemy of your domesticated plants. Plan accordingly with fences, nets, or whatever else you can figure out. Make sure local moose have plenty of their usual food (willow and birch in particular) by clearing as little land as possible. Also note that moose will not eat potatoes (the leaves are poisonous), so most people grow

their potatoes out in the open—and some will plant carrots in between rows of potatoes, hoping the moose don't find them. They usually don't.

- Much of the soil in Alaska is slightly acidic. Plan your crops accordingly, and build soil quality with your compost. You can also lower the acidity by adding the ash left over from your wood stove. Make sure to test regularly, though—you don't want it getting too alkaline, either.
- While the top layer of soil may thaw in spring, soils underneath may stay frozen well into summer, depending on location. The cold soil will really put a damper on plant growth. Using raised garden beds (and cold frames) are a great way around this problem, though they do take some effort to build. Hugelculture mounds will also warm up more quickly. We also use recycled tires as mini-raised beds (let them sit out in the rain for a while before you use them—then they'll be clean).
- As noted elsewhere, let your watering containers warm up with a day's worth of sun before you water—cold groundwater shocks the plants. Water during the afternoon from these containers (barrels, buckets, or whatever else).
- Once you've found out where your worst soil is, reserve it for plants that grow well in poor soil, such as potatoes, radishes, nasturtiums, etc. (and don't forget to build soil quality with compost).
- Rotate your crops from year to year. This is good gardening practice anywhere. A typical rotation might go something like this: peas the first year (to put extra nitrogen in the soil), greens (mustard or kale) the next year, and potatoes the next. Not only is rotating good for soil health, it also keeps certain crop-specific parasites from surviving.
- Too much moisture can be an issue in many parts of Alaska. Make sure your garden areas can drain during heavy rain events. Some people use containers that have holes for sufficient drainage. Old wooden boats make great gardening containers, assuming they have holes in the bottom for drainage. You can also dig your own mini-drainage trenches.

- Keep track of your local climate data—especially the first and last frost dates. I have a neighbor down the hill that has frost much later in the spring and much earlier in the fall because he's in the river valley—I get at least an extra month of gardening time even though we are within yelling distance of each other. Get a thermometer at the very least—a weather station is ideal. Plan for your microclimate.
- Plan your garden location around the existing useful plants (now that you know which wild plants are most useful). The best places to clear are the grassy ones—grass is actually the least useful of the wild growing plants, and (in most places) indicative of good ground. Fireweed is a close second. Even though fireweed is edible and useful, it is also extremely abundant, so you don't need to worry about clearing some in order to plant a garden (the same goes for grasses, really).
- Get a cat or two. They'll hunt the little creatures that want to eat your garden.

Bed 1	Bed 2	Bed 3
Year 1: peas and carrots	Year 1: greens (collard, kale, mustard, lettuce)	Year 1: root crops (turnips, beets, potatoes, radishes)
Year 2: greens (collard, kale, mustard, lettuce)	Year 2: root crops (turnips, beets, potatoes, radishes)	Year 2: peas and carrots
Year 3: root crops (turnips, beets, potatoes, radishes)	Year 3: peas and carrots	Year 3: greens (collard, kale, mustard, lettuce)

Figure 8: Diagram showing a crop rotation scheme for a set of three raised garden beds

Domesticated animals

Everyone with plans for a homestead has their own ideas as to which animals they'll be keeping. Some are standard, like chickens and pigs. But I've had neighbors that fantasized about having a donkey. I don't know why. There was also a guy down the road that wanted to have an elk ranch. That was also perplexing to me. I've known people to keep llamas, yaks, goats, sheep, cows, chicken, ducks, geese, pigs, rabbits, and guinea pigs. Each type of animal has its ups and downs, but the most telling thing (to me) is that I see farm animals given away every year. If you're patient, you'll get free chickens and goats at the very least. This might seem great at first. Then you realize you have to feed them. Then you realize why the previous owners wanted to get rid of them. Winter is long.

If we're going to be practical—and this book is supposed to be about being practical—there aren't really any animals you can keep in Alaska that will give you enough food to make it worthwhile to buy *their* food. Animal feed is not cheap in Alaska. You can grow some of your own, depending on the animal, but you'll be limited by your local climate, topography, soils, and so on. There are, of course, exceptions to my "no practical animals" guidelines. Here they are:

- Musk oxen and yaks: If you have enough acreage and can afford the fences, musk oxen and yaks can mostly feed themselves during winter. They know how to dig through snow to find food. They're tough. They're also good at keeping themselves warm and defending against bears. You can make money on the side by using them as a tourist attraction. No joke.
- Goats: Unlike grazers (sheep, horses, cows), goats are browsers that can eat just about everything that naturally grows in Alaska—willow, fireweed, grasses, birch trees, and even spruce trees. You'd still need to buy food in winter, but they can browse—to some extent—year-round.
- Local feed supply: A couple of locations in Alaska are better suited for keeping farm animals because feed is grown locally and can be bought cheaply. The main area would be Delta Junction, where lots of barley and hay are grown. Other areas with similar crops (but to a lesser extent) would be Palmer/Wasilla, Fairbanks, and the Kobe Ag Project area just west of Anderson.

I tried growing some barley one summer here on the Kenai Peninsula. It didn't work. But we can grow hay, and I guess that's better than nothing. When it comes to dairy animals, the amount it costs to feed the animal makes it so you end up paying more per gallon of milk than you'd pay at the store—except you actually have to feed the animals, milk them, and muck out the barn. I know of some goat farmers down the road that sell their goat milk for $15 per gallon. If they sold it for any less, they'd be losing money.

Keeping animals in Alaska also means keeping them safe. There are wild animals that will want to eat them. We've lost cats to owl predation. We've lost chickens to mystery creatures (eagles?). We lost a duck to a bear. We lost a goat to another mystery creature (some kind of canid—might have been a lone wolf, but the tracks looked more like our neighbor's dog). Most people that keep animals will try to use electric fences, but those take up precious power that might not be available to every off-gridder. We keep our animals in enclosures near enough to the house that the dogs can hear if anything is getting at them. It hasn't been foolproof, but it works pretty well.

The only other thing I want to say about keeping animals is that chickens are unbelievably stupid. They can be a great source of entertainment in this way. I remember watching in amazement as a couple of our chickens stood outside in the freezing rain, sheets of ice growing on top of them, refusing to go into their shelter. Most were smart enough, but not all. We had to pick them up by hand and put them in. More about keeping chickens:

- They sound like they're perpetually preparing for a kung fu battle. I like that. Kung fu battles are great.
- They need roughly 15 hours of daylight if they're going to lay eggs. This means they won't lay in winter if you aren't providing supplemental light. We put a solar panel on the roof of the shed where we kept the chickens, and it fed an old car battery that was dedicated entirely to lighting their little house. It worked.
- They don't need much food in summer but will uproot plants in your garden while scratching for bugs, so beware letting them roam free.
- Eagles will try to take them away. Some people put fishing nets over the top of their chicken yard to prevent this.

No matter the animal type, we have not known of any that actually require an insulated enclosure of any kind (nor have we known anyone who uses an insulated enclosure, and we know a lot of people who keep a lot of different kinds of animals). Whether chickens, goats, horses, or whatever, domesticated animal homes in

Alaska tend to be simple: give the animals a place to gather out of the wind. They have feathers and fur and will keep each other warm if they need to.

Food storage and preservation

When it's harvest time, we have a whole lot of food to deal with at once, whether it be fish, moose, berries, or vegetables. Sure, it's always a good idea to eat as much fresh as you can—no food is ever as good as when it's fresh. But there will be more than you can eat, so plan on saving some for winter. Most preservation methods are obvious: freeze your berries or make jam with them. Greens (including kale) can be blanched (dipped briefly in boiling water or quickly steamed) and then frozen. Most veggies are compatible with canning. Meat can be dried, smoked, frozen, or canned. Root vegetables should be stored in a root cellar.

The real deciding factor when it comes to food preservation is how much power you have. Do you have enough power to fun a full-sized fridge? Chest freezer? These take a lot of energy, and an off-grid power system big enough to keep fridges and freezers going all winter will be very expensive—either that or you'll have to run a generator all the time, which can also be very expensive. So it's a good idea to use other methods as much as possible.

Even so, freezing is a good idea. If you use seasonal power to your advantage, you might have enough energy to run your chest freezer until October or so. If you move it to a shady location (like an outdoor shed or part of a porch or deck), you might be able to just keep it outside and with everything staying frozen all winter (if winter is cold enough). Then when the sun comes back in spring, plug it back in. You can easily keep it packed with ice if necessary (like the old-fashioned ice boxes). We keep a lot of foodstuffs in our arctic entry (where it's usually between 30 and 40 in winter, much like a fridge). We also have an old chest freezer (with the electrics removed) in an outdoor shed.

Root cellars can be tricky, depending on your soil drainage rates and water tables. You might dig a root cellar in summer and have it nice and dry only to find that it fills with water in fall when the rain keeps coming. That water might eventually drain through or it might just freeze in place when winter sets in—either way, slow draining soil can really hamper a root cellar project. A good compromise is to create miniature root cellars by burying waterproof containers (like plastic totes, trash barrels, or even 5-gallon buckets) and having an insulated cover. If you pack your vegetables in straw or sawdust (or something with insulation value), they should last for quite a while. This method is easy and low-risk, so you can try different styles in different locations to find out what works best.

As for canning and smoking, the ins and outs are best covered by books or other publications dedicated specifically to those topics—the methods are pretty much the same as you'd use anywhere else. The only things really worth pointing out are that alder is the preferred wood for smoking meat (fish in particular).

Doing the Math

Living on the southern Kenai Peninsula, we do our grocery shopping in Homer (usually). Sometimes I will see one of the Kilchers at the grocery store. I've seen exactly one-and-a-half episodes of their TV show—I think I must have been at a relative's house (since we don't have TV). I remember the dramatic scene: they were rushing out to Caribou Lake via snowmachine to do some ice fishing because they so desperately needed food during winter. I thought it was hilarious. It takes them much longer to snowmachine to Caribou Lake than to drive a car (less than 10 miles) into town to go to the grocery store. My point is not to denigrate the Kilchers—I'm sure their producers or directors (or something) concocted that entire scenario for an audience that didn't know any better. My point is that a lot of people think Alaskans live more "off the land" than we do.

Over 95% of the food we eat in Alaska is imported from somewhere else (and bought at grocery stores or via mail order). Think about that statistic for a minute. We're *awful* at living off the land. We do export a lot of fish, of course, but that fish belongs to the fishing companies (headquartered in Seattle, largely). And we don't want to eat fish for every meal. But very little of our land is used for growing food, and the popularity of hunting and fishing in the more populated areas means that numbers of moose and bag limits of fish are very low in the places that are easy to get to. I know people that will drive the Dalton Highway all the way up to the North Slope so they can hunt caribou. Sure, it's a lot easier than hunting moose locally—caribou *can* be abundant up there. But by the time you calculate the cost of gas, the time it takes to get there and back, camping gear/food or accommodations, you end up paying a lot for that caribou—probably more than you'd pay for meat at the grocery store.

That's what I mean by "doing the math." Figure out your standard meat prices at the store. Around here that's about $4 or $5 per pound (as of winter 2019—unless you're buying the fancy stuff, and the chicken processed in China tends to be cheaper). Figure out your fruit prices. I know people that will spend hundreds of dollars on getting transportation "across the bay" where the blueberry picking is predictably good. So what are you actually paying (per pound) for those blueberries? Probably a lot more than you pay for other fruit at the store.

Other follies:

- Paying the local meat company to process and package your moose carcass. It ends up being just as much (per pound) as much of what is in the store.
- Chartering a plane to go hunt or fish somewhere that you have much better odds of being successful.
- Having to buy thousands of dollars worth of hunting gear when you'll use it once a year or less (with little chance of success).
- Spending thousands on a high tunnel only to let it get destroyed by winter storms (note: if you have one, you probably want to take the cover down in winter).
- Spending thousands to have your garden area cleared and leveled with a dozer, only to find that you just destroyed its natural fertility and now have to buy a bunch of compost or fertilizer.
- Spending thousands on a chicken coop (I've seen it done) only to give up on eggs because it's too expensive to feed the chickens and to keep their lights on.
- Spending thousands on a barn only to give up on dairy animals because it's too expensive to feed them during winter.

And so on. In short, it's not going to be worth providing your own food unless you can do it efficiently and very near to home. Even so, providing your own food has other benefits. It's up to you to decide if these benefits outweigh the extra cost:

- Eating animals/eggs/dairy that were not fed with GMO corn and/or soybeans.
- Eating fruits and vegetables that were not treated with pesticides.
- Eating food that didn't have to travel thousands of miles to get to you.
- Getting exercise by gardening.
- Having fun on hunting trips because you enjoy it.
- Learning something new.
- Making connections and trading food with local gardeners and neighbors.
- Improving Alaskan agriculture in general and being less dependent on imported food.

And more. In general, it's very possible to get a lot of your food without going to the store, but it takes planning, knowledge, and effort. You may not be able to live completely off-the-land, but don't worry—nobody actually does. Just do your best. It'll be worth it.

Chapter Four: Water

Alaska has no shortage of water—in general. But getting potable water on your property can be very challenging, depending on your location. There are a number of areas where local residents all get their water from the same community water station, and this might be due to the fact that drilling wells is prohibitively expensive in some areas—with no guarantee of good water.

But you planned on having your own river or creek, right? Well, there is waterfront land available out there—but it's usually very expensive (in most areas, anyway). And you'll have to break through the ice to get water in winter. That isn't always easy. Plus, you'd still probably want to treat and/or filter it. I know people that have gotten giardia (beaver fever) from drinking out of creeks. The same goes for lakes. There was a summer in which my wife and I lived in the backcountry on a lake, and we drank lake water—but we either boiled it or filtered it through a *very* high-quality filter.

You may want to keep a map of Alaska handy while reading this chapter—all of these places are well-known to people that live here, for the most part, so I don't think twice when mentioning place names. I apologize if this puts an extra burden on you—but reading it and seeing it on a map at the same time will only deepen your knowledge.

Location, Location, Location

Remember the web soil survey tool I mentioned earlier? Well, that will often have information as to the depth to groundwater in a lot of areas. Apart from looking around on the internet, the best way to find out information about groundwater is to ask locally. The state *does* have a database of well logs on its website, and you can do a map search on this site to find logs for wells near a desired location (just search "Alaska well logs map"). You can also download groundwater data from the state website (if you know how to interpret it). This can give you a general idea, but there are always a number of factors that will influence ground water in any given location. These include soil type, soil layers, topography, and more.

In general, places that are hilly will be difficult for getting a good well. Take the hills around Fairbanks, for example—they are full of dry cabins where residents haul their water from town. The bedrock in the hills makes it very difficult to drill wells, and those that actually get water from these wells are more likely to have high levels of arsenic. The same goes for the hills above Homer—very deep wells with very questionable water (if any water at all). The Copper River Valley is another place with difficult groundwater, which is very deep and tends to be salty. Consequently, most off-grid people in that area haul their water as well. Many rural villages all share a central watering point for ease of access—and also because well-drilling equipment is hard to come by when you aren't on the road system. If you aren't on the road system (and you don't have a body of water on your property), you may want to consider digging your own well—but that's only if you have a water table that will get you to water within 20 feet or so.

There are a variety of ways of digging (or pounding) your own well. Some will use heavy equipment. Some will use a shovel. I used an auger-style posthole digger and added extra pipe to extend it, digging roughly 8 feet down before pounding a sandpoint even deeper into the ground. I've done this a couple of times, actually. Once it failed because I didn't tighten the cap often enough before pounding it down with a sledgehammer (some will use a fencepost pounder—either way, you need a cap on the top of the pipe so you don't destroy the threads). I also broke one of the pipes at a location roughly 6 feet deep and had to leave that sandpoint in the ground—buried it. I have one sandpoint well that worked for a while, but they're tricky—the local silt is so fine that it gets through the screen on the sandpoint and clogs up the pipe. I've pumped some water but ended up putting that project on the back burner. If you want to do your own sandpoint well, make sure you dig deep enough to know your soil layers and make sure the point goes well below any silty layer into some sand and/or gravel.

Areas of more abundant groundwater (in unconsolidated aquifers like those of the Susitna Valley, Anchorage area, western Kenai Peninsula, Tanana Valley, and others) might still have unpalatable water. I've tasted well water in several of these areas that has a tremendous amount of iron. Or the water stinks like rotten eggs (sulfur). Or it might be hard water. So even if you have abundant well water, it still might need to be filtered and/or treated. If you do happen to find a place with a well (or make your own well), be sure to get your water tested—just in case.

A lucky few will have fresh water springs on their property. These can sometimes be developed—but they could also freeze in winter. Either way, a spring on a property is always attractive. Another testament to the importance of soil knowledge: a guy just three miles from me has developed a small stream on his property into a pond simply by using the naturally occurring layers of clay in his soil; this pond provides year-round drinking water.

Hauling Water

If you are one of those that has to haul your water (and you may have to for a while if you're focusing on building at first), you'll need containers and a vehicle to get to and from the watering point. Some people take a collection of jugs. Some people put a giant tank in the back of their pickup (and make it so that any other users have to wait a half hour while the giant tank fills). The giant tank is efficient in one sense—you don't have to fill it very often. But you'll also need a way to pump it out of that tank into another tank at your cabin.

Water at community water stations is treated, so this might not be a good option if you are worried about things like chlorine or fluoride in your water. In our area, developed springs offer an alternative to the treated water—but only for those who know where they are. There are various developed springs all over the state, but most aren't in obvious places (except for that one on the Seward Highway along Turnagain Arm…*everyone* knows where that one is).

Hauling water is not fun. It is tedious. It can get expensive. But it also gives you some perspective: people in many parts of the world have to do the exact same thing, day in day out, for years. And a lot of them don't have the luxury of using a vehicle to transport their containers. You will be that much more grateful when you do finally get a well—or when you develop a rainwater catchment system and cistern.

Harvesting Rainwater

Rain is pretty good stuff. It waters the plants. Groundwater mostly got there from rain (and snow). It's free. It's still not regulated. You can wait for rainstorms and stand outside with your mouth open, looking up. But unless you live in Southeast Alaska (where it rains all the time), that's not going to give you enough water to survive. Plus, you'd probably get hypothermia before you quenched your thirst.

The standard way to harvest rainwater is to use your roof. If you have a galvalume (metal) roof, the rain will roll down with ease and still be clean (though it might have dust and/or pollen at certain times of the year, especially during dry spells). It needs to roll into gutters, then to downspouts, and into containers. Those containers can be buckets. Tubs. Totes. Barrels. I've seen them all used. I've use them all myself. If you have a bit of money and enough time to plan for it, it's possible to divert all of your rainwater into a cistern or a large (1000+ gallon) holding tank. There are a number of people that use this method almost exclusively: rain is diverted to large tanks and pumped out through filters to be used as regular household water. It tends to work best in areas that get more rain.

If there *has* recently been a dry spell, you'll want the first rain showers to clean your roof before you start harvesting water for use—let it wash away any dust or pollen that has gathered on your roof. After that, put out your containers (or open up your containers, or begin diverting to your cistern). Even if you just use rainwater for washing and watering, it will still make a huge difference.

Conserving Water

Water conservation is usually a topic saved for those that live in drought-prone areas. While we do get droughts in Alaska, off-grid types will conserve water mainly because it means you have to make fewer trips to the water station or run your well-pump less often. Both take precious time and energy.

Having hauled water seasonally for a few years, we ended up developing conservation strategies that allow us to get by on roughly 12 gallons a day (20 gallons on bath days). Ten gallons is two standard toilet flushes. The average American uses from 80-100 gallons a day. When we were still a family of 3, we made do with 12 (4 gallons per person per day, sometimes less). Not having a flush toilet is a huge help in bringing down water use (see the chapter on waste for how to get by without a flush toilet). Not taking daily showers helps as well (you can do family baths the old fashioned way: everyone gets a turn, the water gets cooler and dirtier after each use; we add a pot or two of fresh boiling water about halfway through to counteract this). The final big water waster is washing dishes. We obviously don't use a dishwasher. We have a sink with hot, soapy water and a rinse basin with 2-3 inches of fresh water. Before rinsing dishes in the rinse basin, we try to get as many suds off of the dishes as we can. Having the rinse basin keeps us from running water to rinse them one by one—we can just add them to the basin and let it fill up, then empty the dishes into the drying rack almost all at once.

Sometimes people will go to even more extreme conservation measures—like using their gray water to water their garden, or using leftover bath water for pre-soaking laundry. None of these would be surprising to anyone who has lived in a developing country or a drought-prone area, but they might be surprising to some readers.

There are other ways of conserving water that aren't about the actual use of water, but rather about removing the need to use water in the first place. Let's start with a simple one: cups and mugs. When my wife and I drink coffee, we reuse the same mugs day after day for at least a week without washing them. Because we drink it black, there are no sugars left in the mug that could potentially feed bacteria (plus, the hot coffee each morning does a nice job of killing anything there might be in the mug). The same goes for our water glasses—if they've only held water, we don't need to wash them very often. Did the lid to that pot actually get any food on it, or was it just steam? If it was just steam, dry it off and put it back on the shelf.

Think of the way that pioneer types would plan their wardrobe: you have clothes to work in, clothes for school, clothes for socializing, and so on. If I'm going to be doing something dirty or mucky, I'm going to wear rugged outerclothes I save for just those occasions—and I will probably hang them up in the barn, arctic entry, or greenhouse before I come inside. And they will stay there until the next time I need heavy duty clothes for dirty work (they might get washed twice a year or so). I have a different strategy when it comes to clothes for going to work at my actual job. Since I tend to wear button-down shirts for my job, I make sure I always wear an undershirt with short sleeves (as opposed to something like a tank top undershirt). That way if I sweat, the undershirt collects it while my buttoned shirt stays clean. I put the undershirt in the dirty clothes and hang my nice shirt up again. The button-down shirts can go for months without needing to be washed, assuming I rotate them, keep them free of stains, and don't sweat through my undershirts.

Anecdote: The Evolution of a Bathtub

I've met enough people that live the off-grid lifestyle to have had some frank conversations about hygiene. It's definitely an issue, especially because most people start off without running water in their cabin. Some never get running water in their cabin. Because of the self-built nature of most projects, they usually can't be completed in one season. Sure, if we had a whole team of people working on it, we'd have no problem getting it all finished, inside and out, by the time winter sets in. But we are not real estate developers. These are not cookie-cutter tract homes.

Most people—if they know what they're doing—can get a cabin framed and weathered in within a few weeks, weather permitting. Then there's the insulation, interior sheathing, flooring, ceiling, paint, shelves/cabinets, furniture, getting appliances installed, and so on. When you're also trying to get your firewood put up for winter, very few people have time to put the finishing touches on a cabin during the first year. Some never do. We know that a lot of people don't install siding right away (or ever). We may never have trim around certain doors and windows. There might be ugly bubbles of spray foam peeking out from various crevices. We tolerate it because it doesn't affect the functionality of the home.

So a lot of "finish" work goes by the wayside, and that includes plumbing (in particular). Most people make do with some kind of washbasin and water jugs. When that is the extent of your plumbing situation, bathing becomes more difficult than what most people are used to. I know some that bathe once a week or less. Some have told me that they just use wet wipes in place of bathing, and they can go for weeks like that. Some will just head into town and use the showers at the laundromat.

When we first started living in our current location, the situation was the typical one: we had a sink that emptied into a gray water bucket. The sink was fed by a 6-gallon bucket with a little spigot. It actually worked quite nicely for most anything we'd need it for. We had an outdoor shower house that was perfect for summer and fall—a 1000 gallon tank, and inside the little house were a pump and a propane water heater. All of it sat on a flatbed trailer. It helped make our transition to off-grid living a little bit easier. We may not have had much space, but at least we could shower. Until the pump broke. Then there were no more showers—not until the following spring, at least. We needed a new strategy.

At first, we employed the wet wipe method. That worked for a day or two. Then we tried sponge baths. Our oldest was two years at the time, and we started using a big plastic tote for her baths. It was perfect for somebody that size. It was also the biggest open container we had, so we (adults) also tried to use it. That didn't work so well. I couldn't sit down in it. To wash my hair, I had to kneel beside it and dangle my head in the water. For everything else, I had to stand in it and employ sponge bath tactics. It was the same for my wife. After one bath that way, we knew we'd have to do something else. Bathing in the tote would only last until we had that something else figured out.

That "something else" turned out to be a small stock tank. It was a black rubberized thing that held about 40 gallons—roughly half the size of a normal bath tub. Still inconvenient, but a big step up from the tote. We'd have to heat pots of water on the stove (just like they did in the good old days) and fill 'er up. I still had to kneel beside it and dangle my head in the water in order to wash my hair, but everything else was far superior to the tote situation. I could sit down in it. That was huge. And, if I dangled my legs out, I could lay my torso down in it. Good for soaking a sore back. This improved bathing situation created a new difficulty, though: we had to carry it out, full of water, to dump it. No drain. That took two of us, and there was often a bit of sloshing.

I did fix the shower house the following spring. I installed a 12v DC water pump and an on-demand propane water heater—both far more efficient than their predecessors. I powered the pump with a battery fed by a solar panel on the shower house roof. We were back in business (at least we were until freeze-up happened again). This was our method for roughly 4 years: shower house in summer, stock tank baths in winter. That was 2 or 3 years too many, but we were busy with a lot of other projects during that time. It wasn't broken, so we didn't fix it. But it wasn't comfortable, either.

Last year, my wife came across an ad online for an old claw-foot bathtub. A guy up in Anchorage was selling it. Apparently, it had come from the Independence Mine in the Palmer area and was roughly 100 years old—a legitimate gold rush relic. But it was still in fine shape, being an old cast-iron thing that can't really be harmed. She called the seller and was making arrangements to buy it, but we were having difficulty finding time to make it up to Anchorage to get the thing. And while we were trying to make it work, somebody else bought it. It just so happened that the somebody else who bought it didn't even want the tub. He wanted to buy the cargo trailer that the tub was sitting in, and nobody wanted to move the tub out of there, so the tub came with the trailer. Since the buyer was a plumber himself, he was okay with this—he knew he'd find a use for the tub at some point.

We lucked out. The seller got us in touch with the guy who had bought the tub. He lived only about 25 miles from us and he was happy to sell it to us. We paid the same amount we would have otherwise, except we didn't have to drive nearly as far to get it. He helped us load it into our pickup and even sold us a drain fitting for it—he had plenty of them in his work truck. It took a while to get the tub cleaned up, and getting the drain situation figured out took a couple of very frustrating tries, but it works. We can now take baths in which we can fully lay down in the tub. We don't have to kneel down to wash our hair. We can drain the gray water to the outside.

We feel like royalty in that thing. Four years of uncomfortable baths will do that to a person.

Water and Winter

Water freezes when it gets cold enough. That means it doesn't flow. That also means it expands (and if it is in a confined space, this expansion will probably break whatever is confining it—such as a pipe). If you have any outdoor water tanks or plumbing, make sure you drain them and/or bring them inside before the first hard frost. In this sense, living off the grid and hauling water is nice: without plumbing, you don't need to worry about pipes bursting. You don't need to worry about clogged toilets. You don't need to worry about anything overflowing.

If you get your water from a creek, river, pond, lake, or spring, you may be worried about ice making it hard to get your water. Some will break through the ice to gather what they need (which gets more and more tedious as winter wears on and the ice grows thicker). Some would rather haul their water from a regular watering point. Some will even just melt snow and ice and be happy enough with that. If you have a well, make sure your water line is at least 6 feet below ground level. The ground will typically freeze at least 4 feet deep in any given winter (sometimes more or less, depending on your location). If your water line isn't deep enough, the ground will freeze around it and the water will freeze inside of it—creating some real problems.

If you harvest rainwater, you may want to take your gutters down in winter. Heavy snow loads can cause them to buckle and/or break. However, you can leave them out if you are diligent in keeping them from snow buildup. Then, during the occasional warm spell, you'll have water flowing again from the melting snow (or during a winter rainstorm, which seem to happen more and more these days).

So while you may not be able to use bigger water tanks and abundant free-flowing water in winter, you may not need it so much—you won't be watering your garden, you won't be needing as many showers or baths (not working and sweating in the heat), and you won't be as thirsty. Just keep your containers inside and enjoy the simplicity. You're not trying to impress anyone, so relax.

Laundromat as Off-Grid Social Hub

Since so many of us haul water (at least for part of the year), the local laundromat becomes the de facto social hub for the off-gridders. Even some of the on-grid crowd will end up there in the wintertime because of frozen pipes, or in fall time because the rain caused their septic system to back up. The good laundromats will also have showers. Our local one does. It's a one-stop place for a good dose of civilization, complete with wifi and a mini café.

It's akin to the saloon of the old west. You'll find random old-timers sitting and shooting the breeze, cups in their hands. There will be plenty of talk about weather and any notable gossip. Don't be surprised to hear a good conspiracy theory or two. If you have questions about how to do anything related to off-grid living, go hang out at the laundromat for a while. There will be someone that has answers for you (it might even be me). Just don't be put off by our appearance. We look scruffy but are always happy to help.

Chapter Five: Waste

Waste is often the last thing people think about when they plan a homestead in Alaska. Most don't think beyond the stereotypical outhouse. Waste is an issue for two main reasons:

- Outhouse holes fill up in only a few years.
- Even the most "sustainable" homesteads still have a lot of waste that is not easily recyclable or compostable.

Trash

It's easy to get used to having someone else carry your trash away every week. Trash is unpleasant to deal with. It stinks. Depending on what you put in there, it might distill down into a garbage juice that permanently sloshes around in the bottom of your trash can. It doesn't *have* to be permanent, but nobody has the guts to clean it out, so it stays. If you live somewhere hot, it fills the house with a rotting stench. It doesn't *have* to be awful. Ours isn't. It rarely stinks because we don't put anything stinky in there, for the most part. (This argument sounds suspiciously like one used by my former stepmother: she literally claimed her poop didn't stink because she was a vegetarian. She was wrong.) And we do take it to the dump at least once a week. We're on the road system, so that helps. But road system or not, all of these tips will help you keep your trash to a minimum—and at minimum stench.

- Collect kitchen compost and be prepared to dump it into your compost bin at least weekly. For us, this is stuff like coffee grounds, banana peels, and any food waste that isn't fat/bone/meat/dairy (though some people compost that stuff as well, if their pile is hot enough. You can also add bits of cardboard, paper, etc.—it will all break down. Add it to the rest of your compost material for a huge pile of future fertilizer.

- Use your pets to take care of any food waste that can't be composted. Our dogs will eat just about any leftover food, plus any bones that we aren't using for soup. If they're pokey bones that might not be good for eating, they go in the trash or we use them for spells, potions, or making creepy little sculptures that we hang from trees to scare off any tourists that might be wandering around. Kind of like that Blair Witch, you know?
- Get a burn barrel for cardboard and paper trash. Or just keep this stuff in a little box by the wood stove and use it for starting fires.
- Reuse anything that can be reused. We have zippered food storage bags that are over 5 years old. We just wash them and reuse them. Old coffee cans are great for storage. Eventually you'll look for reusable or burnable packaging when you're deciding what to buy at the grocery store. The internet abounds with ideas for reusing stuff.
- Your remaining trash will be minimal—mostly tin can remains and various plastic packaging. This isn't usually smelly and doesn't accumulate very quickly.
- Tie up your trash bags and keep them in your arctic entry—or perhaps in the bed of your pickup (if it has a cover/canopy). Don't leave it outside. It'll bring the bears. Or the coyotes. Or the porcupines. Or the weasels. Or the ravens, crows, and magpies. Or the flies.

The 55-gallon Drum

If you can get an empty metal barrel or two (the 55-gallon size), you can turn them into burn barrels or use them as containers for your outhouse hole. If it's a used barrel, make sure it's clean first. Often these barrels were used to store gas or diesel fuel. If there are still remnants, find a safe place to put the barrel, then throw a match in and stand back. Let any residual fuel burn off. You don't want that stuff getting in your groundwater. It's much better to put it in the atmosphere (it was going to end up there anyway if it had been burned in an engine, as was its purpose). I'm not even joking.

If you plan to use it as a burn barrel, you will want to put holes in the side—especially on the lower part. Otherwise, your fire will lack oxygen and will not burn well. If you plan to put the barrel in an outhouse hole, you'll want to put holes in the base. This will allow the liquid waste to filter out so that the outhouse hole fills up more slowly.

How do you put holes in these barrels? Well, some people would shoot them, but I don't recommend this. If you don't do it right, there could be ricochet and/or sparks. I prefer the mattock. If you don't know what a mattock is, it is very much like a pickaxe. One side is very pointy (like a pickaxe) while the other side is a flat blade (like a garden hoe but thicker and stronger—it can also be sharpened for things like cutting through roots). You pick up the mattock and swing the pointy part hard at the barrel. It will make a hole. Don't swing sideways—hold the mattock above your head and swing downward like you're chopping wood.

The Front Yard is a Salvage Yard

For many of us, trash that can't be burned, composted, recycled, or taken to a landfill simply sits in the yard. Jeff Foxworthy would like to make a joke about your yard, but it's no joking matter. A lot of these defunct items might come in very handy some day. A quick scan of our own yard is a good reminder. We don't think about this stuff because we see it every day, but it's laying around and it's useful. We have a pile of hoses (various sizes). We have miscellaneous pieces of fence material and fence posts. We have leftover roofing metal and flashing. Various lengths of PVC in various diameters. Pieces of gutter for future water projects (or backup). A defunct wringer washer with a perfectly good wringer in it that will replace the one on our current washer when it finally goes out. Floor mats from old vehicles. Side mirrors from old vehicles. Old clam shovels that might get put to use when clamming opens up again. Tires of various sizes—some used as planters, some just hanging around. Scrap wood. Old metal barrels that will be used for burn barrels or outhouse receptacles one day. An assortment of cement blocks. Tarps. In-laws. Buckets.

Most people will also have an old 4-wheeler or snowmachine or and old passenger vehicle or two—all good for parts in one way or another.

Of course, that's all just stuff that can sit out in the weather and not get too terribly damaged over time. The stuff in our barn and sheds would yield a similar list—but more specifically would be things that are more susceptible to mold or rust, things with more moving parts, smaller things that need to be kept in containers, and so on. We have bikes and punching bags and extra siding and "better" scrap wood and tools and camping gear and leftover insulation and shelving brackets and that old chest freezer that doesn't work anymore but it keeps things nice and cold during winter without having to be plugged in. You see? It's just not practical to throw this stuff away. It's useful. We're not hoarders—I have every bit of confidence that everything will be used eventually. In fact, we take great pride when we look through the scrap building materials and find uses for scraps in our various projects. It's a good feeling.

This all has the extra added benefit of keeping yuppies out of the neighborhood. Not that they'd want to live with so few comforts to begin with, but like I mentioned before: this type of Alaskan yard art is a point of pride for some. We don't judge. And by keeping up these appearances, we ensure that we won't get neighbors that *do* judge.

Human Waste

Very few places in Alaska are served by sewer systems. Certain villages have them. Certain cities have them. For the rest of the state, the options are very limited. Septic tanks are a possibility in many areas, but that assumes the soil is compatible with a septic system (many soils are not, and soil perc tests are required before installing a septic system) and that you can get a septic tank to your location (which means these systems aren't a possibility for more remote sites). Many people that *can* have septic tanks still don't have them because it can cost upwards of $30,000 to get one installed. So if you don't have a local sewer system and can't have a septic tank, what options do you have?

The classic Alaskan answer to this question is an outhouse. An outhouse can certainly have a rustic appeal, and some people take them seriously enough to design "classy" outhouses with cedar (to keep the smell down), shingle siding, magazine racks, and so on. They are simple enough to make, but they do have a few drawbacks. The first is that a standard-sized outhouse hole (to fit your 55 gallon barrel) fills up after a few years or regular use, or maybe even sooner (depending on your dietary habits). Then you have to move your outhouse to a new location, and this is a giant pain. Digging the hole can be easy—done in less than a day if you have nice, soft soil. But some soils do not cooperate with your shovel. Then comes the actual act of moving the outhouse. It is typically dragged (they sit on skids for a reason), and this might require a 4-wheeler, a draft horse, a winch, or other tools. If it hits a snag during the dragging process, it might tip over. That happened to one of my neighbors. It was not fun. Not for him, anyway. It was a *little* bit of fun for those of us that tried to give advice but were ignored and got to watch him do it the wrong way and fail. I'm pretty sure I hid my laughter (but it doesn't matter because that guy moved away anyway). Outhouses can also be very cold in the winter, and many people put foam board insulation on top of the toilet seat to keep it from freezing to skin (or just to make it less cold to the touch). There are also many stories about people getting trapped inside of their outhouse when a bear comes by at an inconvenient time—so they sit for a while until it is safe to go back to the cabin. That can require tremendous patience. It is not the most pleasant place to have to wait on a bear. They are curious creatures and rarely in a hurry.

For many, a better solution is to use a composting toilet. It has many benefits when compared to an outhouse. For starters, it doesn't have to be outside. That's a big plus in the winter. There are two types, really—commercial and homemade.

Commercial composting toilets can be pricey, sometimes upward of $1000, but that can be easily rationalized when one considers that the materials for an outhouse cost many hundreds to begin with, and a composting toilet doesn't have to be moved intermittently. Some of them require additives, some of them burn the waste (incinerator toilets), and all commercials models require some kind of power to operate. This can be accomplished when one is running a generator, or it can come from an alternative energy system.

Homemade composting toilets require no energy, but they do require occasional labor—about 10-15 minutes per week. Instead of the composting process happening inside the toilet itself, the toilet simply acts as a collection device and is then emptied into the main compost pile once full (this is where the composting takes place). The materials required are few when compared to an outhouse, they are a lot cheaper compared to a commercial composting toilet, and they end up providing you with more "bang for your buck" in terms of good compost at the end of the process. All you need is a standard 5-gallon bucket, a toilet seat (you can buy ones that fit perfectly onto a bucket, or you can build a small wooden frame to sit around the bucket and support the seat), compost bins (which you should already have), and carbon-rich cover material such as sawdust, dead leaves, dead grass (straw), shredded paper, or even dirt. There is an entire village near Kotzebue that uses this system as a way of dealing with both human waste and shredded paper waste.

You can combine this with your regular kitchen compost for ideal nutrient balance. The end result (after a pile composts for a year and then rests for a year) is rich compost that will nourish your soil. For more info, see *The Humanure Handbook*, by Joseph Jenkins. There are a couple of Alaskan modifications we discovered that aren't mentioned in the handbook.

- Keep your bucket in a room of the house that doesn't freeze. For a few years, we kept our bucket in a shed. It would freeze into a giant poopsicle that didn't want to integrate with the rest of the pile. We ended up with a pile of poopsicles in the compost bin, eventually, and had to add a whole lot of boiling water to the pile during winter just to melt the ice that was taking up *way* too much space. Sometimes we'd chip them down with a hatchet. Yes, just imagine seeing people swinging small axes at frozen cylinders of human waste. Not our proudest moment. You don't want to have to go through that.
- Some of your compost pile will freeze during winter, but the center will stay active if you're adding to it at least weekly (and the stuff you're adding isn't too cold when you add it). In this case, you can just break the top off of the pile (use your shovel as a lever to make it "hinge" until it breaks free) and slide it over like a manhole cover, then dig into the unfrozen area underneath. It's fascinating to watch the steam rise once you move the lid. That bacteria is still hard at work digesting everything—even in the dead of winter.
- Once things start to thaw a little bit in spring, you'll want to find a time to tend your compost pile before things really

start to get warm. You might see egg shells that fell off the pile in winter, or various other things—take this opportunity to put anything that belongs in the center of the pile back into the center of the pile (underneath cover material and exposed to the heat of the pile).

- A well-maintained and properly covered pile will not stink at all. If it stinks, you're doing it wrong. If it's visited by birds or other animals, you're doing it wrong. Read the handbook again. Our compost bins have never been a nuisance when it comes to wildlife. There were a few nights one fall when a porcupine found a raspberry patch we'd planted very near our compost bins. He ate our raspberry plants but didn't touch the compost (and then my wife waited in ambush one night and emptied a revolver into him, saving the rest of our raspberry plants).
- Add some fish carcasses to the pile during salmon season. These will improve the fertilizer value of your compost. Last summer we added a dozen or so, and the heat of the compost pile became so intense that we opened up the pile a few days later to find the fish bones had entirely disintegrated. Think about that: the bacteria in a good compost pile can digest bones in a matter of days (or *don't* think about that if you happen to be someone who is planning a murder—it probably wouldn't work on bigger bones like human ones, anyway). This is why you don't see anything but dirt when you finally put the compost on your garden: no little pieces of cardboard. No banana peels. No eggshells. And certainly no toilet paper. Everything broken down into its most basic components: nitrogen, carbon, calcium, phosphorous, and so on.

If all of this sounds too technical, you could just use a shovel and poop in a hole (when the ground isn't frozen). In fact, I once knew a guy that didn't have an outhouse, a septic tank, or a composting toilet at his off-grid cabin. You know what he did? He used plastic grocery bags. When he was done, he tied the bag up and put it in the back of his truck and then took the pile of bags to the dump once a week or so. It wasn't legal. And it *was* disgusting. But it worked. Woe to any dumpster divers that came across his deposits…

Gray water

For cabins that lack a septic system (as most off-grid cabins do), there is the question of where to dump your gray water. Gray water is what is left after you wash your dishes, have a bath, and so on—water, yes, but not necessarily *clean* water. The state has limits as to the amount of gray water that is permitted to be dumped—laws that were created for temporary situations like logging camps. Most off-grid homes should be well below this limit, but they are also inhabited year-round.

Some solve the gray water issue by creating a leach field. It is basically the same thing as a septic system but for gray water. The water goes into a holding tank that slowly releases it into the leach field (area of land where the soil can absorb and filter the water); the little bits of sediment float to the bottom of the tank and stay. That would also include the bits of food left after washing dishes, etc. These systems would pipe gray water out of the house, which is nice because gravity does the work for you.

What most of us end up doing is to keep a bucket beneath the sink. When the bucket gets full, we take it out and dump it. But because we care about our soil, there are some measures we take to make sure the gray water isn't harmful to our soil:

- We take all food waste off our plates before washing dishes. Vegetable matter goes in the kitchen compost bucket. Non-compostable food goes in the trash or to the dogs.
- We only use biodegradable/natural soaps and detergents.
- We don't dump a bucket in the same place twice.

Some people will dump their gray water down the outhouse hole. That's a good place for gray water to go—but beware of splashback.

I'm sorry…is that one poop joke too many? I've become desensitized to talking about it. Once you've lived off grid for a while (especially if you have small children), it stops being disgusting and becomes just another fact of life. It happens. If we weren't okay with being intimately acquainted with it, we'd move somewhere with a sewer system. You can't have it both ways. I'd rather it be funny than disgusting. Don't let poop have so much power over you.

Chapter Six: Heat

Hey, guess what? Alaska is cold. It even has a reputation for being cold. We may complain about it being excessively warm at times (and getting warmer), but it's still colder than most places. The Midwest will often be colder in terms of temperature (in winter), but the main difference is that our winter lasts longer. If you did a good job designing and building your home, there's a good chance you won't need to heat it from late spring thru early fall. But that's less than half the year. Heating a home for 7+ months can be a huge undertaking, especially because almost everyone that lives off-grid uses wood as their exclusive source of heat. It's possible to use a propane or oil heater if you live near enough a place to get your tank(s) refilled (or if you are on the road system in a convenient enough location for a truck to deliver these fuels). A lucky few might even has a natural gas pipeline nearby. Those don't require much planning or strategy, and don't really need to be addressed here—you just buy your fuel and burn it, the heater doing everything automatically. Heating with wood, however, is an art in itself. It requires a lot of hard work cutting and transporting the wood, but it also requires planning for kindling, rotating your wood piles/sheds, properly seasoning wood, and, of course, building fires.

Building a Shed for Firewood

When we talk about firewood, we use the term "cord" to measure amounts of firewood. A "cord" is how much wood it would take to fill a box that is 4 feet by 8 feet and 4 feet high—128 cubic feet. Different parts of Alaska require different amounts of firewood to get through a winter. In many parts of Southcentral Alaska, 3-5 cords is enough (or even less, if it is a mild winter). In parts of the Interior, you will likely need upwards of 10 cords per winter. In some areas—Delta Junction, for example, where you not only get Interior cold but also regular strong winds coming through the mountains—you'll need even more.

If you plan to build a single shed for your firewood, plan the size so you can fit at least a full winter's worth inside with a little extra space (you'll want air to flow through the shed and between the pieces of wood). A shed that fits 4 cords would need to be 8x8x8 at the very least (preferably a bit bigger). For 8 cords, that would be 8x16x8; 12x12x8 would give you just a tiny bit more space). For 12 cords, you might as well just build a big barn and be done with it.

You'll want all sides covered to keep snow and rain off of your wood. Some people prefer 3-sided sheds—that makes it easy to carry wood out with both arms and not have to worry about opening or closing a door—but you'll want it extra big so that the wood is stacked far enough back from the open side for moisture to stay off of it. Again, you'll want airflow so that your wood stays dry and continues seasoning as it sits.

Some people stack their firewood on the ground and cover it with tarps. This can work, but it is less convenient than having sheds. Plus, the tarps will sometimes blow away during a big storm. Then you'll have *really* wet wood.

Getting Wood into Storage

One way to get around having to build a huge shed (or several smaller ones) is to cut wood continually throughout the winter. This will only work if you know which wood to cut. If you plan to burn wood right away, your only option is to find a standing dead tree—one that has been dead for long enough that the moisture has left the tree and it can be burned right away (or you can find a *leaning* dead tree, but be careful cutting those—they can pinch your saw; also don't bother with dead wood that is lying directly on the ground, as it is probably too rotten or soggy to be useful). Trying to burn green wood (from standing *live* trees) is a bad idea for a number of reasons—particularly because it doesn't burn easily (it can be frustrating to start a fire, and you might not have the luxury of time when your house is cold) and it creates extra creosote in your stovepipe (which will then require more regular cleaning).

Be strategic when choosing which trees to cut. Consider what is surrounding the tree:

- Are there a lot of other trees?
- Will it be able to fall to the ground without getting caught on other trees?

- Is the area around the base of the tree clear of brush? You'll want to be able to move out of the way quickly when it starts to fall.
- Is it too big to be practical? Think about the size of the rounds once it has been bucked. Rounds from a very thick tree will start to feel very heavy after you've been carrying them to and from your sled or shed for a while.
- Are you contributing to a healthy forest? Think about cutting trees that are close to other trees on only one side: the two (or more) trees are competing for the same resources (nutrients in the soil, water, and sunlight). Cut the smaller, weaker tree—assuming you can get it to fall away from its neighbor(s). The neighboring tree(s) should benefit.

In general, smaller trees are better—it makes for an easier task. Cutting and transporting the tree won't take so much of your day. You'll need to cut more of them, yes, but you'll have plenty of time to get the ones you need.

I won't bother describing the process of cutting the tree down. That is better shown with instructional videos or in books specifically about tree felling. But know that you should make a notch, then cut just slightly above the level of the *base* of the notch on the opposite side of the tree. Don't try to get a tree to fall in any direction other than the one it is already leaning. Some can make that happen. My grandfather and great uncle used to play games with each other when they worked as lumbermen—daring each other to fell a tree so that it landed in a specific place, or even telling the other one to stand just far enough away so that the tip of the tree landed at his feet when it fell. Leave that kind of thing to the pros. You don't want to get badly injured when emergency medical help might take hours to get to you (or you to it). Play it safe when it comes to chainsaws and felling trees. I will sometimes use an axe for cutting trees, but only when I want to waste extra calories and feel like Abe Lincoln.

Once the tree is down, it needs to be limbed (the limbs cut off) and then cut into sections before being moved. There are two ways to do this: cut it into the longest sections you can comfortably carry (so you move as few sections as possible) or cut it into stove-length pieces right away. Regardless, this process is called "bucking."

Which you choose will depend on the situation. When we cut trees very near the house (within a couple of hundred yards) during the warm season, we will keep the sections as long as possible and carry them over our shoulders back to the yard before cutting them into stove-length sections. If we are pulling a sled with human or dog power, we will cut the tree into the longest sections that comfortably fit in the sled. If we are using a 4-wheeler with a trailer, we will cut the tree into short sections right away. Make sure that you cut straight through (across) the log when making sections—try not to have any angle to the cut. This will make it a lot easier to split later on.

Note: when I say "stove-length" sections, I mean pieces that can comfortably fit in your stove. There is nothing more frustrating that trying to put a too-long piece of wood into a hot wood stove. You won't be able to close the door, which can lead to an excess of oxygen on the fire (and potentially an "overfire" situation). So to avoid that you would remove it immediately, but part of it might have already caught fire. It's not fun to run through your house with a giant flaming torch, trying to get it outside before too much smoke gets in the house. Practice cutting wood to the proper length. Remember that thicker pieces will need to be shorter.

The best time of year for cutting firewood is spring (before breakup). Shrubs, weeds, and grasses will all (ideally) be under a layer of snow, or at least beaten down by winter to an extent that gives you better visibility. Cut on cold days when the snow is nice and firm—this makes for the easiest transport by sled. We cut our wood locally enough to drag a sled by hand (or by dog), though some people prefer a snowmachine (especially if they have to travel longer distances). After you've felled/limbed/bucked the tree, load it in your sled and take it home. It might take several trips. Once home, finish the bucking process. You may also want to split it right away—splitting firewood is easiest when the temperatures are cold (in the teens at the very most, but zero is fantastic).

If you're lucky enough to find trees you can cut right by a road, you can just load your truck bed with wood directly. That's the quickest and easiest. But the places you can easily (and legally) do that are getting fewer and fewer, as is the case with *any* resource that you can drive an automobile to. You can always count on people being greedy and lazy, so plan for it.

Storing and Seasoning Wood

If you aren't cutting standing dead wood only, you'll need to season it. No, don't sprinkle it with salt and garlic. Seasoning means to let it sit for a year (or even two) before you burn it to give it a chance to dry out. Sometimes you can get by with just seasoning wood for a matter of months—but this would require the ability to tell if it's already partially seasoned. After you've dealt with enough firewood, you can tell if a piece is seasoned or not as soon as you pick it up. It has to do with weight and density: if a piece feels too heavy for its size (if it is too dense), it is not yet seasoned and still needs to lose some moisture. It doesn't take too long to develop this skill.

Each person has his or her own system for stacking and rotating wood. We like to keep a variety of different shapes and sizes in the shed (and in the wood rack inside the house) so that we always have the right piece of wood for the fire in any given situation—this means big split pieces, small split pieces, big un-split pieces ("rounds"), small rounds, and kindling (more on this under "Fire Building Strategies"). There is endless debate as to the proper way to stack pieces of split wood: bark side up vs. bark side down. Each has its advantages. Try them both out and see what works best for your situation.

You'll also need a way of stacking wood so that it gets rotated. If the back of your shed is full of wood and you stack wood in front of it, yet you don't burn through enough to use that wood in the back of your shed, it will sit for extra years. This might mean extra seasoning (which can be good), or it might mean that it starts to get punky (spongy) and rot. If you have extra space in your shed (which you should), you can work around this problem by stacking it in a horseshoe or u-shaped manner—you can walk into the center of the shed and grab wood from any side at any time. You might have the left side dedicated to round pieces and the right side dedicated to split pieces, or any other method that works for you. We solve this problem by having multiple small sheds—one dedicated to split pieces, three more dedicated to round pieces (each being at different points in the seasoning process), and a space in the barn for emergency backup wood. When the shed with split pieces starts to get low, we just split rounds from one of the other sheds and move those pieces to the split wood shed after they are split.

You'll want another dedicated space for kindling. As you split wood, you'll find that a lot of small pieces are created in the process. These should be stored and saved as kindling. Small branches that you cut from logs before bucking them can also be saved for kindling. You'll also want to collect birch bark whenever possible. Birch bark is the best material for starting fires—period. Just make sure it's dry. When we have split birch pieces, I make an effort to peel the bark off and save it for kindling. If you come across downed birch logs too rotten for firewood, you can still take the bark off for kindling. Having a good supply of birch bark will make your fire building process a lot faster and easier. Just remember: don't peel bark from live birch trees. It can kill the tree.

Of course, newspaper and cardboard are still great for starting fires, but you might not have a steady supply of it.

Fire Building Strategies

Start by reminding yourself that fire needs three things: fuel, air, and heat. You'll need to know how to use all three to your advantage if you plan to heat your home with wood.

Most people outside of Alaska (and even most people in Alaska, for that matter) don't heat their homes with wood. The forests of the more populated places are shadows of their former selves (like I said earlier: if you can drive a car to it, people have been cutting firewood, legally or not). Other heating alternatives are cheaper. In some states, regulations restrict the kinds of woodstoves a person can use so that there are few options (and expensive ones, at that). But most of us should be familiar with starting a campfire (if you have never started a campfire, you should probably stop reading right now and go try camping a few times before you think any further about moving to Alaska). Campfires are simple: you start with kindling and build upward, often in the popular teepee shape. Some papers or shavings in the center (at the bottom), tiny sticks above that, larger sticks above that, and maybe even a decent sized piece (though you want to save the big stuff for later, after the fire is going). These are simple because air is abundant and the fire moves vertically, always burning upward, from the smallest pieces to the largest. The small stuff gets going, lights the slightly larger stuff which gets going and lights the slightly larger stuff, and so on.

Wood stoves don't work quite the same way. You have to plan your fires differently because of a number of factors:

- Air is not as abundant. It comes into the stove through a specific (adjustable) opening, the damper.
- The location of the opening will determine the direction of the air flow. While the air still moves upward, it usually moves laterally (horizontal) before going up.
- Because there is much less air than in a campfire situation, you must compensate in the "fuel" and "heat" categories in order to get the fire going well.
- The temperature of the firebox might not be the same as the surrounding air. There also might be a plug of cold air pressing down from above.
- The air pressure can be different between inside and outside the house.
- The smoke needs to go through a specific opening. If you haven't installed your chimney correctly, smoke might try leaving through other less-desirable openings (like the cracks where your sections of stovepipe come together), flooding your house with smoke. This might also happen during certain weather events depending on chimney height, wind speed, wind direction, and atmospheric pressure.
- You can't just put a giant log in a woodstove and expect it to burn all night. Your fire will probably need tending.

Because of these factors, it takes practice to master the art of wood heating. Furthermore, every stove is different, and every setting is different, so each stove is *its own* art form. Mastering your own wood stove won't make you an expert at your neighbor's place (though understanding the basics will serve you well anywhere).

The flow of air: Find the point at which the air enters your woodstove. Think of this point at the bottom of your teepee. Build your fire in reverse. For example, the air comes into my woodstove through a little opening at the bottom of the front of the firebox—right in the center (very common). It exits the firebox through a much larger opening at the top of the front of the firebox. But the air doesn't just go straight up the front of the firebox—the shape of the opening forces the air, upon entering, to move toward the back of the firebox first. As it moves back, it spreads out (think of it as sort of a V-shape). When it hits the back wall, it moves up. When it reaches the top of the firebox, it must move toward the front before it can exit. After it is above the firebox, it moves to the rear of the stove again before exiting through the pipe at the top of the rear of the stove (see the diagram that follows).

With that in mind, I start by putting a medium-sized piece of split wood along the back wall of the firebox. Because split wood is wedge-shaped, I am able to lean other pieces of wood easily onto the wedge (it also helps if I have something very small underneath the front lip of the wedge so that it isn't laying flush against the bottom of the firebox—that helps a little bit of air get underneath the wedge as well). I'll put bits of cardboard or birch bark at the bottom of the firebox directly in front of this wedge. I will lean slightly smaller pieces onto the wedge at an angle (they lean over the cardboard or birch bark). In front of those I'll lean slightly smaller pieces interspersed with crumpled paper. And in front of that might be the smallest of all pieces and even more paper. If the air is very cold outside, I'll add a couple of pieces of paper to the top of everything, but loosely—this isn't meant to feed any kindling, only to burn by itself.

Now that the fire is ready to light, follow the flame at it comes from my match, then follow the flow of air as it spreads the fire:

1. I light the loose pieces of paper sitting on top of the fire. These will burn themselves out quickly. That's fine. Their purpose is twofold: to heat the firebox itself and to get the chimney to start drawing air through the system (this heat can help break through any cold air plugs that might be sitting in the chimney). Sometimes people prefer to burn paper in an empty firebox a few minutes before building the fire. It serves the same purpose.
2. As the loose pieces on top begin to burn, I bring the match down to the paper at the very front of the fire—right in front of the opening where the air comes into the firebox. This paper lights and the flame starts to move from the front center of the firebox toward the back, spreading as it goes.

3. As this paper burns, it begins to ignite the tiniest pieces of kindling on top of it. It also ignites the pieces of cardboard and/or birch bark behind it.
4. As the kindling, cardboard, and birch bark ignite, they will light the slightly larger pieces of wood that are both behind the kindling and above the birch bark/cardboard.
5. As these larger pieces burn, the airflow continues to carry the flame to the back of the firebox, and these largest pieces of kindling should be large enough (and burn long enough) to get the split piece at the back to catch. Once this bigger piece is going well enough, you can relax (though you will still be tending it for a while yet).

Of course, this will take several minutes, but the air flow is continually taking the heat, air, and flame from the smallest pieces (at the front) to the largest pieces (at the back). This is why I referred to the point of air entry as the "base of the teepee": it's where you put the tiniest pieces, the kindling, the paper. And the process I just described is what I meant by building your fire in reverse. With a campfire, you start with the tiniest pieces and build up. With the wood stove, you start with the largest pieces (at the point farthest from where the air enters the firebox) and build progressively smaller until you get to that air entry point.

Keep in mind that not every stove design is the same, but remember these principles:

- Find the path that the air takes through the stove.
- Put the smallest pieces closest to where the air comes in and the biggest pieces farther away.

Those will serve you well with any stove.

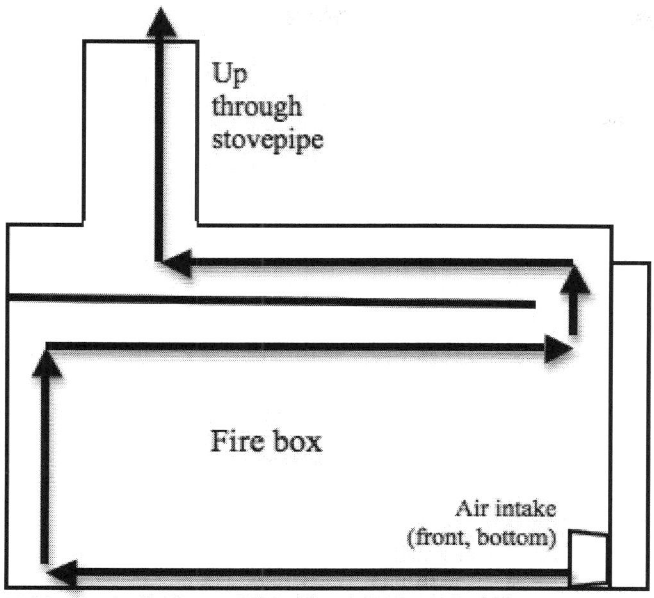

Figure 9: Typical air flow in a wood stove

The control of heat and fuel:

Once your fire is going, you'll use the damper to control the amount of air that comes in. The more open the damper is, the more air comes into the stove. This means the fire will burn faster and hotter. By using the damper in conjunction with proper wood selection and placement, you can get the most heat out of the least wood.

The first thing you need to do is to get your fire up to a temperature that is self-sustaining. That means it is burning hot enough that you could put any piece of wood on the fire—even a dense round—and it will burn to completion without needing a lot of smaller pieces in with it. This is the point at which you may consider closing the damper a little bit to conserve wood and keep your house from getting too hot (which can happen).

Many people will keep the stove door slightly ajar as the fire is in its early stages. This allows extra air into the firebox and it can be very handy in that way. There are only a couple of downsides to doing this. First, if you leave the fire unattended with the door open, the extra air might cause the fire to get too hot and you can end up with an overfire situation. Second, the air coming in from a different location might not be compatible with your fire design. Because the main source of air has changed, it might seem easier to arrange your wood and kindling in a way that anticipates air flowing in through the open door. But you'll eventually be closing that door—hopefully after only a few minutes—and you'll want to make sure your fire design fits the situation for the rest of the time.

Once your fire is going and hot, it is time to make choices. What to burn? Well, how cold is the house? If it's really cold and you want it to heat up quickly, you'll want to burn split pieces, and smaller ones at that. Pieces with the greatest amount of surface area relative to the overall volume of wood will burn faster and hotter. Different types of wood burn hotter as well. Birch burns hotter and earlier than spruce (these are the two main types of firewood you'll be using in most parts of the state, though you might also have some aspen, cottonwood, or alder), but the heat doesn't last as long. Spruce doesn't have as dramatic of a burn profile—it burns at a steadier heat for longer. So heating your house up quickly should be done with small, split birch. Maintaining heat should be done with larger pieces (and more spruce than birch).

You may also burn aspen, cottonwood, and alder, but these are less common. Aspen is a lot like birch. Cottonwood is very porous—not very dense compared to others—so it burns quickly. Alder is usually smaller and a bit of a pain, though it is more commonly burned just because it's abundant and grows quickly—people are always cutting it down just to get rid of it. It is also the wood of choice for smoking salmon. None of these (not even the birch or spruce) would be considered "good" firewood in the lower states. They don't burn as long or as hot as woods like oak, beech, or hickory that are sought after elsewhere. With that in mind, be aware that the you'll need more wood in order to get the same amount of heat you'd get from those more desirable types. We just have to cut more wood to get the same amount of heat, since our most common types do not burn as hot or as long. That also means we have to spend more time tending our fires.

As a general rule, we burn rounds once the fire is hot enough to allow it. First of all, this means we didn't have to expend any energy in splitting the rounds. That's a plus. Second, we don't need to feed the fire as often. Rounds burn more slowly for a couple of reasons—they are more dense than a split piece of comparable volume, and there is less surface area (in relation to volume) that can burn. This also allows us to keep our damper wide open for longer (less tending).

There is debate among wood burners as to whether it is better to burn wood at a slower pace for a longer time (by partially closing the damper) or burn wood in hotter, shorter spurts with the damper completely open ("batch" burning). They both have their advantages. Burning at a lower temperature means you will probably have a steadier temperature in your house—the closest thing you'll get to having a thermostat—but the low temperatures will mean more creosote will accumulate in your stovepipe. Burning wood in hot bursts will keep creosote from accumulating as much, but you'll have to be okay with bigger temperature swings. (We have a friend whose stove automatically (electronically) adjusts the damper in order to maintain a steady temperature—a wood stove with a thermostat. It's a great stove, but it has to be plugged in 24/7—so not a practical option for most of us living off-grid.)

When getting ready for bed, most of us have a preferred protocol for loading the stove up with wood so we don't have to wake up every couple of hours to add wood. This will depend on your stove's capacity. If it is a large stove, you can load enough wood to burn through the night. But having a large stove in a small house is not a good idea (it can just make the house way too hot). Our stove is on the small side. In fact, it might even be too small now that we've added on some extra rooms. If it is a cold night, I will typically add a small-to-medium sized split piece near the front of the firebox and a couple of rounds above and behind that. The smaller piece will burn long enough and hot enough to make sure that the rounds will burn through without needing to be tended. The direction of airflow takes the heat and flame from the smaller piece to the bigger, denser ones. I close the damper slightly, but not too much—a little less than halfway, usually. It burns slightly cooler than usual but I don't have to worry about the fire dying for lack of air. This method might keep the fire going well for 3 or 4 hours. Even if I don't wake up by that time, there will usually be some coals smoldering in the ash when I do get up, and restarting the fire with hot coals and a warm firebox isn't too hard. But with the warmer winters we've been having lately, I can often just load the firebox up at bedtime and then not bother to add anything during the night. The fire goes out and the temperature drops, but it usually doesn't get below 55 or 60 before it's time to wake up, and that's not too bad.

Of course, you'll have to tend the fire regularly when the wind is blowing heavily. The wind will suck heat out of your house long before the ambient temperature does.

Troubleshooting Your Fire

Fire not starting well? Not staying lit? As you learn the ins and outs of heating with your wood stove, you'll want to ask yourself these questions if things aren't working right:

- Does the fire go out after a few minutes?
    - You do not have sufficient kindling to light your larger pieces (and to keep them lit). This is a problem I sometimes have, as I try to build fires using minimal paper and kindling (my instinct is always to conserve material).
    - Having to add more kindling after the fact will be less effective and it will also cause smoke to come into your house.
    - When in doubt, go a little overboard. A little extra kindling will not hurt your fire, but too little will keep it from reaching "escape velocity" (what I call the temperature threshold when it begins burning well on its own with the door shut).
- Does the fire not stay lit after you have closed the door?
    - Check the damper. Is it open all the way? If not, open it and see if that's enough.
    - If a fully open damper is not enough, open the door a crack and let more air in.
    - Monitor the stove temperature and close the door once you've reached the threshold temperature (which you should memorize).
- Is there excessive smoke or lots of hissing?
    - Your wood got wet. It happens sometimes.

- Instead of taking a smoldering piece of damp wood out of your stove, you may want to just add some smaller pieces that will burn hot and quickly—that way you'll just evaporate the moisture away.
    - To prevent this from happening, make sure your wood is well covered in the shed.
    - You can also feel if it is heavier than it should be due to extra moisture. If it feels too heavy for its size, don't put it in to begin with.
- Was your fire going fine, then suddenly went out?
    - The pieces probably shifted in the stove and settled in a position not favorable to airflow.
    - Use your poker to make sure that pieces are all close to each other and that air can still pass between them.
    - Sometimes this can happen when smaller pieces burn out and leave large gaps between pieces. Again, adjust them so that they are closer; that way the pieces can feed off of each other.
- Did your fire burn out completely?
    - If there are any coals remaining, layer new pieces on top of them, making sure that they are above and slightly behind the coals (in relation to airflow).
    - In this case, start with smaller pieces, then slightly larger above and behind those.
    - If there are no coals, start a new fire if needed. Check that ash buildup isn't blocking the airflow.
- Can't see through your wood stove window to tell how well the fire is doing?
    - Scrape your window with a razor blade.
    - There is a spray that is supposed to work for this, but it doesn't work as well as a razor blade.
    - Burn hotter fires and the haze on your window will burn off.
    - Having a clear window is very helpful in fire maintenance.
- Is the window rattling?
    - The window gasket needs to be replaced.
    - Replace it.

- Does the door not seem to close all the way anymore?
    - The door gasket needs to be replaced.
    - Replace it.
- Did you foolishly wedge a piece of wood into the stove that is too long for the stove but it's already on fire and you don't want to take it out and you can't really budge it, either?
    - Don't do this. Learn to use a measuring tape.
    - Consider putting the fire out and starting over (the officially safe thing to do).
    - I know of people that will just monitor the fire closely, then close the door once enough of the piece has burned to allow for some shifting of the wood pieces. I cannot officially endorse this, as keeping the stove door open for too long can lead to overfire (an overfire is when too much oxygen gets the fire so hot that it actually damages the stove—it can warp metal or even create holes in the stove).
- Is there smoke leaking through the little cracks where the stove pipe joins together—or through any other little cracks?
    - Your stove is not drawing properly.
    - Make sure the damper is fully open.
    - Open a window (preferably two) to help equalize the air pressure between inside and outside the house. This will also help clear smoke away.
    - Your stove pipe should be cleaned as soon as possible (once every 6 weeks or so is a good idea).

If your fire is frustrating you, just remember: if you have good fuel and enough heat and oxygen, the fire *wants* to burn. It's amazing to see how some fires progress—there might be a collapse that results in horrible airflow, yet the flame will often find a way to break through. The most common cause of wood heat headaches is poorly seasoned or wet wood. Make sure you have quality fuel and you'll enjoy making fires.

Other random tips:

- NEVER use any kind of lighter fluid to get your fire going (that includes gasoline). I know of two cabins in this area alone that have burned down in the past 5 years specifically because of that. It's very dangerous.

- When you go to the dump, check the cardboard recycling bin. Lots of good fire starter material there…
- When using corrugated cardboard, separate the layers as best you can (peel them apart). This will increase surface area and make it better for getting a fire going.
- Use a long-stemmed lighter, if possible. Matches will sometimes break or go out before they can light anything. It will just save on frustration.
- Get a combination smoke detector/carbon monoxide detector. They're not too expensive, they run for a very long time on a single battery, and you'll have more peace of mind.
- Always have a fire extinguisher handy around the cabin.
- If you have a stack fire (chimney fire), throw a bucket of water into the stove (and step back quickly). The steam that results will go up the chimney and put out the fire.
- Get a fan to help circulate the heat. There are a number of models available that don't require electricity—they just sit on top of the stove and the heat from the stove causes the fan to spin.
- Make sure your wood stove has a thermometer. You'll want to monitor the temperature regularly. Pay close attention to the temperature at which the fire can easily continue to burn under its own heat (after starting). Memorize this temperature (it can fluctuate depending on the wood you are burning, but it will usually be pretty close).
- Get a trivet or two to sit on top of your stove. Then you can keep pots and kettles on there. It won't work for regular cooking (it heats very slowly), but can be good for simmering a soup or heating water for coffee, tea, or washing dishes.
- If your woodstove doesn't have a grate for the wood to sit on, consider adding a couple of small pieces of firebrick (or something else that can take the heat) for your wood to sit on. Your fire will burn better if air can circulate beneath the wood.

- Recycle your woodstove ash. In winter, spread it on icy ground for traction and faster melting (instead of sand). Spread it on garden areas that are too acidic (test your soil before and after). Or you can combine it with diluted urine to make a potent fertilizer for your garden (look it up to find out the correct proportions—it's supposed to be the best fertilizer there is!).

Keeping the Heat Inside the House

Since you're now well aware of the time and effort that goes into heating an off-grid Alaskan cabin, you'll appreciate that heat and take measures to conserve it. Apart from construction measures for heat conservation mentioned earlier (i.e. few windows on the north wall compared to south, sufficient insulation, etc.), here are some other tips for keeping that heat where you want it to be—inside.

- While you may have a specific "arctic entry," you may want to have other additional rooms added as a buffer at each exterior door. For example, we have an arctic entry at our west entrance, an attached greenhouse/sun room at our south entrance, and another entryway at the north entrance.
- Having curtains/drapes/shutters can actually slow heat loss through windows.
- If you're going outside (or into the arctic entry) for anything, consolidate your trips so you don't need to open and close the door as many times.
- Consider using thermal mass to help maintain heat through the night—this would be something like a stone fireplace or a large container of water: something that will absorb heat while your fire is burning, then slowly release heat after the fire has gone out.
- If you can, get innovative—look into ideas like rocket mass heaters (not easy if you live far out, but worth it if you can make one) or circulating hot water in pipes that come and go from your stove.
- Make sure your home isn't losing heat through big cracks or holes (get familiar with spray foam). Some air circulation is good, and you'll want air moving through the house—but

you'll want to use windows for that, if possible, so that you'll have greater control over it.

- Put siding on your house. A lot of people in rural or suburban parts of Alaska leave their houses un-sided (you can see the white house wrap from a great distance). While this might keep some of the weather off of the exterior sheathing, it's not as good. Siding helps keep the cold from penetrating the house (especially the wind) and it's one more layer to slow the escape of heat.
- Do you like baking? Do your baking on the coldest days. The extra heat from the oven can really help out.

Dressing for the Weather

Alaskans like to joke about being tough. We brag about 40 degrees being t-shirt weather. Actually, it *is* t-shirt weather, especially in spring when you've been used to much colder temperatures. Just because we can tough it out doesn't mean we should. In other words: if it's cold, put on a jacket. Keeping yourself warm is even more important outside than it is inside. People do get hypothermia and die.

You will probably be doing a lot of things outdoors in all seasons. That's the way things go, and it's a good thing in the long run. Wearing the right gear at the right time can keep you comfortable and prevent frustration. You'll want a very good raincoat—one that keeps the water out no matter what (get one a little bit on the long side). You'll want boots that don't leak—regular rubber boots for most of the year and good winter boots for the cold times. Comfortable feet and hands make it possible to get outside work done in any weather. Have strong socks that are at least partially wool. Get some good fingerless gloves or mittens. I like the mittens with the flap that folds back. Mittens are a lot warmer than gloves, so I'll have the flap folded back when I need to use my fingers, then fold it back over again and let my fingers warm up. Hats are essential, but beware of hats that don't let your head breathe. My favorite hat for even the coldest weather is just a basic knit stocking cap. Sometimes it will grow a layer of frost on the outside, as the moisture moves out and then freezes. That's okay. The inside is still warm and dry.

Many people will buy a ridiculously large winter coat full of goose down or something similar. While this is a good thing to have for extreme cold, it's not practical for most days. I can be comfortable in a much thinner jacket in temperatures down to -30, but that includes wearing polypropylene underlayers (military surplus ones are the best) and keeping active as long as I'm outside. Your body produces enough heat to keep you warm. You just need to make sure your outermost layer keeps the wind out and the warmth in. Having an in-between layer that wicks moisture away from your body is helpful. In fact, I often have to unzip my coat about halfway when I'm out walking in deep snow or doing something strenuous—it's essential to getting that heat and moisture out so that I don't start to sweat. Sweating in the very cold is a bad thing. Then you are wet. If you stop moving, that wet will start to get cold in a hurry (and it might even happen while you are still moving).

Dressing for the weather applies to being indoors as well. It's okay to wear a sweater inside. I do it all the time. Have a blanket on your couch and keep it over you when you're reading. Have multiple comforters on your bed. Have some house slippers. If you can comfortably tolerate a colder inside temperature, you'll save yourself a lot of time, energy, and money in the long run. You'll also appreciate your hot meals and drinks a lot more.

Chapter Seven: Energy

Why bother with electricity, anyway?

I recently saw a meme on Facebook that serves as a great introduction to the philosophy of energy usage.

Wait, you mean I'm not supposed to look at memes on Facebook if I live off-grid in Alaska?

Tough. I love a good meme.

Anyway, the meme was something along the lines of this: there was a picture of some NASA people—they might have been astronauts or they might have been mission control people. I can't remember, and that part isn't important anyway. The words on their picture noted that 4kb of RAM got them to the moon. It was contrasted with a picture of a teen girl with some Instagram filter that made her look like a puppy. The words on that picture noted that she was using way more RAM for…making herself look like a puppy. The moral of the meme is supposed to be something like this: don't waste valuable resources on stupid crap.

Before you go and plan your off-grid energy system, take some time to evaluate what you use your electricity for. Is it stupid crap? Are you going to put 15 grand into your solar power system just so you can keep watching Kardashians while in the backwoods? It's worth mentioning because I've seen it happen. I've seen people spend a fortune on their homestead (and power system in particular) just so they can live exactly like they lived in the lower 48, complete with satellite TV. If that's the case, why did they move here to begin with?

Who knows.

As you take stock of wants and needs, you'll find that it's quite freeing to classify most of your power usage as "unnecessary." You can rebuild your life based on needs, and use the lack of easily available electricity as a good excuse to cut out all of the stuff that's been bugging you for all these years. You don't have to waste that time anymore, and now you have a system for keeping yourself accountable: you simply won't have the power to binge watch whatever the guilty pleasure TV show du jour might be (that time saved will be used in other ways—see the "Transportation" chapter).

When it comes to energy usage in my house, it's fantastically simplified: we *need* to run a refrigerator, some lights (except for in summer), and phone chargers. That's it. The rest? Just wants. Electric mixer? Not a need, but it makes for better baking. Laptop charger if we want to use the computer (whether for typing things like this or watching DVDs). Charging headlamp batteries for outside meanderings during the dark times. Vacuuming when it's a sunny day (but we could really just beat our rugs with a stick like they did in the old days). And the ultimate luxury: modem and router for internet…except that we don't always have enough power to run it when we want. That's the point. I have to skip past those bad memes and focus on the good ones. I have to make the most of my browsing when we have the power to do it.

Batteries

Batteries are the basis for any off-grid power system—even those that rely heavily on generators. Buy deep cycle batteries (some people prefer 6v, some prefer 12v) and connect them in series and/or parallel to create a 12v or 24v system. From this battery bank, you can run lines directly to DC-powered appliances like refrigerators and lights. You can connect the batteries to an inverter and use the inverter for standard 110v AC power (the kind that uses outlets you are familiar with). Or you can use a combination of DC and AC power (this is what I prefer).

It looks like this: DC Loads←Batteries→Inverter→(breakers)→AC outlets (each arrow represents flow of energy through cables). Power runs from your battery bank through cables to your inverter (for AC power) and/or DC loads (like a fridge). The inverter is usually connected to a breaker box that distributes the power to AC outlets in the house, but not always.

Regardless, you'll need to charge the batteries if you are going to be drawing from them to power your home. The three main ways that people charge their battery banks are generators, solar panels, and wind turbines. Apart from making sure the batteries stay charged, you also need to make sure they are maintained—keep distilled (and *only* distilled) water handy to top off your batteries (you'll need to open the tops of the batteries and look inside—make sure there is liquid up to the rim and that nothing inside the battery is exposed to air, assuming it is a standard acid battery). Don't let them drop too low in voltage. Don't let them get too cold (they don't perform as well). Keep all cables and connectors tight (loose connections can start a fire). Keep terminals clean. Even with good maintenance, a battery bank is not likely to be very effective after about 5 years, so be prepared to buy new ones when the time comes (and make sure you recycle your old batteries or dispose of them properly).

Some nuts and bolts:

- If you have 6v batteries, you use two of them to make a 12v battery by linking them in series: connect the positive terminal of one battery to the negative of the other. The remaining terminals (one positive, one negative) would be what connect to your inverter and/or DC cables. This same principal can be used to use two 12v batteries to make a 24v battery (in case you want to run a 24v system).
- If you have more than one 12v battery (and you should probably have more than one), connect them by using parallel jumpers: one cable connecting the positive terminal of one 12v to the positive terminal of the other, and a second cable connecting the negative terminals of the two batteries together.
- Use super heavy duty cables.
- Use the shortest cables possible: DC power diminishes over distance. This is good to keep in mind for cables coming in from your solar panels, etc. (anything that is DC power).
- Get batteries with the tallest terminals you can find. I have a couple of terminals that barely hold everything that is on them. You'll want the type with nuts that screw on to the terminals.
- Keep a volt meter handy for checking each battery.
- If you are using a wrench to loosen or tighten a nut on one of the terminals, make sure that wrench doesn't touch other terminals in the process. If the wrench is touching a positive terminal and a negative one simultaneously, sparks will fly.

- Keep your batteries in a place where there is good air flow (and not inside of your house proper). They can vent out some stuff that you don't want to breathe in. We keep ours in a box (with holes in it) in one of the Arctic entries. The room has a couple of vents, plus the door is getting open and closed regularly, so it works well. Some people will have a dedicated shed just for their batteries and/or inverter and generator.

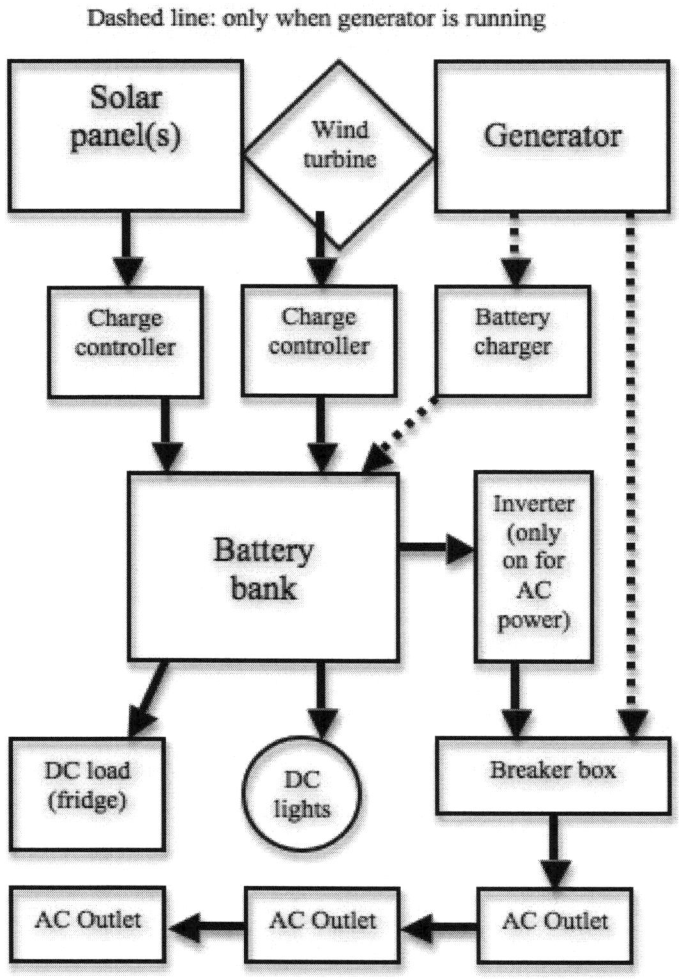

Figure 10: Typical wiring for an off-grid power system

How many batteries? What kind of inverter?

Since these questions will really vary depending on the size of your house and how much power you plan to use, there is no single answer. At our house, we use four deep cycle 6v batteries and a 2500 watt inverter (but again, we conserve our energy). Most small houses would end up needed a 3500 watt inverter (and/or generator).

The best way to figure it out is to write down everything you plan to use (i.e. appliances). Look up how much power they draw (the info can be found online). Think about what different things might be running at the same time, like having an electric mixer, computer, and AC fridge running simultaneously. Once you've figured out the maximum amount you'll need, add a little more just in case. That will tell you roughly what inverter to buy. This is the method I used and it hasn't failed me yet.

If you have a heavy load running off of too few batteries, they will drain quickly and you'll be left with weak batteries and a lack of power. It's better to have a little bit too much battery power than too little.

Generators

We all start the off-grid experience by running a generator—it's simple and reliable, for the most part. Some people never move away from the generator. I know people who have lived off grid for years and run a generator every single day. That doesn't seem to bother them. It would bother me. I don't want to have to haul that much gas. I don't like the constant noise. Even so, they're something you need in case of emergency regardless of how much you use it the rest of the time.

I could write about what size you need. I could write about which brands or types are most efficient or reliable. What you buy should depend on how often you plan to use it. If you plan on running one all the time, you might want to get one of the inverter style generators—they tend to be more efficient and quiet. Another good strategy for those that run them regularly is to charge your battery bank with generator power as long as the generator is on—then you can turn the generator off for a while and run other things (like those essentials) on your battery power.

It looks like this: AC Power←Generator→Batteries (each arrow represents flow of energy through cables). Plug your AC power *and* a battery charger into the generator. The batteries get a break from running things and get a boost from the generator. The AC power runs as it usually would (there should be a cable that can connect your generator to the breaker box). Once your batteries are nice and full, turn off the generator and run things on battery power.

Some people go big and invest in an industrial-size diesel generator. This is actually a decent idea if you plan on using a lot of electricity—but keep in mind that they're more expensive and very large. They need their own shed or trailer, usually. Whatever kind of generator you have, you'll need to get familiar with it.

- Know how to check the oil (and change it, if possible—it's very much like doing it on a car: out with the old, in with the new). Spark plugs, too.
- Have a couple of gas cans to make sure it will always have fuel when you need it.
- Most people keep their generator in a small, vented shed. This helps it stay dry and it will function better.
- Don't overuse the choke when starting it.
- Some generators have a little switch to let fuel through from the tank. This will need to be in the correct position for the generator to run.
- Never run the generator inside your home (not if you're living in it). People die from carbon monoxide poisoning by doing this.

Solar Power

Solar power is nice because it's easy. You buy solar panels. You put them up. You plug them into the charge controller (solar cables and plugs are extremely easy to connect—you don't need any expertise at all). You connect the charge controller to batteries. You are done. That was easy, right?

Right.

It looks like this: Solar panels→Charge controller→Batteries (each arrow represents flow of energy through cables).

The obvious nice thing about solar power in Alaska is that there is plenty of it in summer. The not-so-nice thing is that there isn't very much in winter. I recommend mounting solar panels directly on the south-facing wall(s) of your home. It might not be the ideal angle for summer light, but sunlight is so abundant during summer that it really doesn't matter—you'll always have plenty, assuming you have a decent sized solar array. It *does* happen to be an excellent angle for capturing sunlight during winter with the extra added benefit of not accumulating snow. A neighbor just down the road from me has a very nice and large solar array set up at an ideal angle for year-round use. But he gets no solar power after a snowstorm due to snow covering the panels—but I do. And if your solar array is in a hard to reach place (and they're often high up, on roofs and such), it might not be so easy to brush that snow off in order to get your solar panels going again. Mounting panels vertically on a wall is also nice because you don't have to worry about poking a hole in your roof (and potentially creating a leak). For that matter, you could just use them directly as siding and save yourself some money in that way.

How many panels do you need? How big should they be? Poly or monocrystalline? Series or parallel? There's no single answer, obviously (like with the inverter, it depends on the size of your house, the energy you use, and your local climate). We have 900 watts worth of solar panels—two 150 watt panels and five 100 watt panels. For our family of four, that (combined with our 450 watt wind turbine) keeps us in power year-round without having to run the generator more than a few times. But we also conserve electricity more than most. Since this book is (once again) about being practical, it's worth mentioning that the entire system cost less than $3000 (including panels, cables, charge controllers, mounting hardware, batteries, and inverter). It's not uncommon for people to spend 15, 20, or even 25 thousand on their solar power system—but these are situations when they go directly to a solar power retailer/installer and buy everything as a package deal—including installation. Designing and installing it yourself can save a lot of money.

There are also less obvious pros and cons to solar power. Pro: no moving parts to break. Con: trees might block your sun—and trees keep growing, so you may need to keep clearing trees in order to keep getting power (which might not be possible if you are close to a property line and your neighbor doesn't want to be helpful). Pro: extra solar power during summer can be dumped into extra (backup) batteries. Con: panels can break—beware of hail and flying tree debris during storms. Pro: solar power keeps getting cheaper and cheaper (except for during a trade war with China). Con: Alaskan weather can sometimes be gloomy for weeks at a time.

Wind Power

It just so happens that there are often storms during those weeks and weeks of gloomy weather. With storms come wind. Having a wind turbine (or two or three) can be essential to keeping your batteries in good shape during cloudy times. If you live near the coast or a mountain range (and most Alaskans do), you'll have regular wind anyway. You might as well let the wind give you electricity while it does its thing.

It looks like this: Wind turbine→Charge controller→Batteries (each arrow represents flow of energy through cables).

The most difficult thing when it comes to wind power is finding a good place to put it. You don't want any obstructions (like spruce trees) nearby. You want to make sure it's higher up than anything in the immediate vicinity. In some areas, that can be pretty tough to do. Some people need to buy tall towers and stabilize them with guy lines in order to get the necessary clearance. There's an easy answer to the clearance problem: put it in the immediate vicinity of your cabin. The area around your cabin should be free of brush and trees to begin with ("defensible space" in case of things like wildfire, which do happen). This clearance should be increased (especially on the south side) if you have solar power. You should probably increase the clearance to the north as well, since winter winds will often come from the north (winds that can bring you electricity), and you'll need wind power more in the winter than at other times of year.

Wind turbines typically mount on 1.5" diameter pipe. This can be on top of a stand-alone tower, anchored to the ground with cables. For us, a 14' section of pipe sits right beside the house—it is screwed into a flange bolted down to our deck, and the pipe itself is stabilized by a bracket that connects to the outside rafter. The wind turbine only sits a couple of feet higher than the roofline, but that's all it needs. With no obstructions in any direction, it catches any wind we want it to. For much of the year, that means we keep it turned off. We don't want extra wear on the bearings. Because of its proximity to the house, it can also get noisy—so we typically shut it down before bed unless we desperately need to charge our batteries.

We also turn it off when the wind gets too strong—it shuts itself down (temporarily) when a gust of 35 mph comes, so we don't bother keeping it on if the wind speed continually ventures above 30. This particular model is DC, so having it very near the battery bank helps conserve energy. Some turbines are AC—if you plan on having a wind turbine mounted to a tall tower that is not immediately next to your house, you'll want an AC model.

Other Renewable Energy Systems

Water power is not very practical. If you have a creek or small river on your property, it might be nice to run seasonally, but it will probably never pay for itself. And when everything freezes, it will just sit there.

There have been a couple of biomass generation projects in the state, in which biomass (wood products, basically) is burned to create electricity. These are not doable on a small scale.

A very lucky few are able to use geothermal power. If you happen to live right above or next to a hot spring, you can use the heat from the spring in any number of ways. Of course, buying land with a hot spring is not possible for most of us, either—it's very expensive.

Does that mean that we're only able to use generators, solar, and wind power? Pretty much. And that's okay, because we don't really need that much power anyway.

Anecdote: Learning Off-Grid in Ireland

My much younger self used to travel all over, perpetually on tour as a singer-songwriter. I did this for many years. These travels took me to every state, much of Canada, and much of Europe as well—the UK and Ireland in particular. During one of these trips, I arranged to take about a month off and work on a farm in southwest Ireland. It was one of those WWOOF things—I'd volunteer my labor in exchange for food, a bed, and education. This particular farm boasted being run entirely by alternative energy sources: solar, wind, and water. It looked like the perfect place to learn.

Getting there was actually very tricky. The nearest town (slightly less than 5 miles from the farm) was very small and had no bus service. In fact, there were no public buses in the region at all, at least not during that time of year (it was fall, after most tourists had gone). I could have tried hitchhiking. I'd tried that in the area once before. It didn't work so well. I'd had a show on a Sunday and again, no buses were running to the place I needed to go. It had started raining after I'd started down the road, and I had to give up after a couple of hours and walk back toward Killarney and then somebody finally picked me up. I'd missed the show, so I had the guy drop me off at a friend's house just outside of town. No, I wasn't going to hitchhike there again. But I found an alternative: there were still tour packages being sold for bus trips around the "Ring of Kerry." Not a public bus line, but it could work. Tourists were meant to ride the bus the entire time, make regular stops for refreshment, listen to the guide's presentation about the history of the area, and arrive back where they started. The driver wouldn't notice if a passenger disappeared from the tour part way through. Or maybe he would notice. It wouldn't matter to me either way.

That's exactly what I did—I hopped off in a small town and started walking, just me and my backpack and my mandolin. After about an hour, I found the farm (clearly marked) and walked up the drive, looking for signs of life. It was lovely. It sat in the middle of a small valley, hills on either side, mountains in the farther distance, and a stream running right through the center. Everything was still green, being September, and the temperature was still warm (by local standards, at least). There were various structures on the property and I couldn't tell what was what. I didn't know where to knock. But I did find a younger man outside, explained who I was, and followed him across a footbridge up to the main house. The owners showed me my place in the bunkhouse (which had no electricity) and gave me a tour. There were several gardens, several high tunnels (they called them "poly tunnels," which is probably a more common name for them), and several houses. People had a habit of coming to the farm to work, then liking it so much they wanted to stay, so the owners let them build their own places. I smelled a cult.

I turned out to be wrong—there was no mention of religion from anyone on the place. Just regular people that had become friends and saw no problem with wanting to live near friends. I ended up getting to know most of them well, but not the owners. After I was only there for a day or two, they left for vacation, only returning a day or two before it was my time to depart. But on that first day, I got my first lesson: one of the wind turbines was malfunctioning. We had to take it down, and that was not going to be easy. It was on its own tower, stabilized by guy lines. That meant we needed to replace the guy lines with other lines of similar tension. These were ropes through pulleys, a third line going through a winch so the tower (which had a hinge at its base) could be let down slowly and easily. Even with several people and the right tools, it was nearly a disaster. Lesson one summary: wind turbine towers can be a giant pain in the rear. And wind turbines will *all* eventually need some kind of maintenance.

Apart from direct instructions for a couple of small projects (like leveling a spot at the top of a small hill and putting a water tank there for a future gravity-fed water system), I was told where the food was and whom to go to for instructions—and was then left to my own devices. I was expected to work for eight hours in a day and I planned to honor that. There was one other volunteer worker, a French guy who spoke decent English, and he'd tell me what to do about regular farm duties. The rest of the time I'd be helping one of the tenants, Tom, build his house.

There was only one time in which there was a big enough rain to merit turning on the water turbine. The creek needed to be quite swift and swollen for it to be of much use in terms of generating electricity. Lesson two: water turbines need to be in ideal locations in order to be productive. There are reasons that the early water mills tended to be located near small waterfalls.

While I didn't learn much about installing and using alternative energy, I learned a lot of other things.

I learned that chasing and catching chickens is tedious.

I learned how rotating compost systems worked.

I learned that most electricity use is wasted. The only things that were used regularly were lights and refrigeration (though I also learned some extra French by watching French-dubbed episodes of *Lost* during many evenings). All of our other entertainment was more traditional: we played music in Tom's house or at weekly guitar club meetings. I took the dog for walks around the area and in the hills. We spent occasional evenings in the local pub, where UB40 was perpetually playing on the jukebox. I read books. We even had a big party on the property. All leisure time was centered on personal artistic enjoyment, social relationships, or both—there wasn't the general passive consumption of media that I see when I visit people in the lower states. And I loved it. It was fulfilling, even though I was a stranger to everyone.

I learned how to cut custom pieces of lap siding to fit perfectly around windows or other odd features. Tom's house must have had 8 or 12 sides or something—very geometric. It was really nice, and the natural edges on the siding gave the whole place a very "traditional cottage" feel. I learned how to hang doors. I learned that people that live in rainy places will keep working whether it is raining or not (growing up in a dry area, I'd been used to people hiding indoors during rain events). I liked that. I learned that the work day goes by quickly when you stop every hour or two for a cup of tea and a snack. Yes, we had elevenses every day. I became quite a fan.

Most of all, I learned to love my quiet evenings alone. I grew fond of cooking simple dinners for myself. I would walk around and eat fresh berries for dessert, pulling them right from their bushes. I would stand in the gardens and watch the sun set over the hills and feel like everything was perfect. The only problem was that it was going to be temporary. It wasn't *my* farm. But I could have something similar—someday. I'm still working on that and getting closer every day.

Conserving Electricity

I previously mentioned that, at our house, we use DC power for lights and refrigeration. This is helpful, and it serves as a compromise: we *could* get a regular-sized AC refrigerator. We *could* wire our house with AC outlets and have regular lights and light switches at familiar places on the wall by a door. But to do so would requite upgrading our power system to a size that, while prohibitively expensive for us, would also bring up that same question hinted at earlier: If we want to live like that, why are we off-grid in Alaska? We come here to simplify.

When you come to an energy dilemma, you must ask yourself: Should I spend more money on solar panels and wind turbines and batteries, or should I find a different way of doing this? Because there are different ways of doing things. Having DC lights is a compromise. When we have weeks of gloomy, calm weather (little sun or wind), we can choose to run a generator to charge our batteries so we can run our lights. Or we can light candles. Usually we light candles. And we go to bed earlier and sleep longer. As for the fridge, I already noted that our arctic entry stays between 30 and 40 degrees during the cold season. If that doesn't keep enough food cold, we have that old chest freezer sitting in a shed. If the weather isn't cold enough to keep that at the right temperature, we could harvest ice and pack it in there. We could make our own giant ice cubes by leaving open containers of water out at night (don't leave closed containers of water out to freeze or the containers will crack).

If you have the time and resources to plan around minimizing energy use, you'll find that there are still old-fashioned ways of doing things that work well—like using candles. Instead of running an electric well pump, you could use a hand pump. My wife likes to sew. If we wanted, we could get a foot-powered sewing machine (I've seen them advertised locally…the only problem is that those ones take up a lot of space). Instead of a coffee machine, you can use a French press. Instead of using a propane stove (and especially instead of having a stove you need to plug in), you can use a wood cook stove (we have one of each). We have a hand-crank coffee grinder. You can get hand grinders for making your own flour. The list can go on, but the strategy is the same: look at what people did before everything became electric. An ice box packed with ice. Wood cook stoves. Candles.

Speaking of candles, there are ways of making them more potent. We have several candle mounts at strategic places along our walls. These mounts have mirrors that reflect the candle light throughout the room, doubling their potency. What's more romantic than a candlelit cabin? There's a fire in the wood stove. It's warm inside. You have your slippers on. It's dark out, but the wind is calm. It is quiet. There is no generator running. Just the sound of snow falling. This is what we want. Less, not more.

Chapter Eight: Transportation

There Are No Freeways

Nope. Well, there are in Anchorage, and for a little ways toward Wasilla, but Alaska doesn't have the kind of roads and transportation system you'd find elsewhere. There is minimal public transport. The train system doesn't go to many places and is expensive for passengers. Few cities have public buses, and they don't venture out of town. There are public ferries in many areas, but they are very slow and don't run in bad weather. That means we all have to have our own cars or other motorized vehicles. Things are spread out. It'd hard to get around without gas power of one kind or another. Sure, there are a few hardcore types that do without it. I've seen a guy that rides his horse to and from town. Of course, that can only work in these warmer parts of Alaska. Horses don't do well in deep snow. There are some people that use dogsleds, but then you have to feed a dog team—not an easy thing to do if you don't have a fish wheel or easy access to a large, salmon-bearing river.

Whatever the case, you will need a way to get supplies to your place regularly. You *will* run out of food. You *will* need more gas for your generator, or more propane for your stove, or more candles for light. Even old Dick Proenneke didn't just stay put in his cabin for all those years. He had regular deliveries via float plane. He would fly out and visit people. Even the most self-sufficient people need human contact. Even the most self-sufficient people need new tools every now and again.

Human-Powered Transport

Humans have been getting around pretty well for a long time—a lot longer than internal combustion engines have existed. The first Alaskans got here by walking. It works. You walk and you carry things that you need to carry. Hooray for bipedalism! You might also use a pack or a sled. You might need snowshoes. But walking has always gotten the job done.

Regardless of whether you have vehicles, it's a good idea to maintain a trail system around your place. These might be trails to your gardens, to your berry patch, to a river or creek, a stand of firewood, or anywhere else you might want or need to go. This might require some clearing—nothing that clippers and a manual weed-whacker can't manage. Once you've keep a trail clear for a year or two, it will stay trodden. The plants won't grow back as long as you keep using your trail regularly.

Once snow falls, you'll need to keep using your trail system. Keep using the trails after each successive snow so they stay packed down and hard. You may need snowshoes from time to time, but that's kind of fun in itself. Having trails that are clear and packed means you can go anywhere under human power at any time of year. In winter, that might be on foot, on snowshoe, on ski (some people are serious about cross-country skiing—most do it for fun, but some use it for transport), or on bike. A growing number of Alaskans ride "fat bikes." They are specially designed to be ridden on snow and ice. The tires are oversized with aggressive tread and are often studded. If you need to haul firewood, take some snowshoes and a sled. If you need to get to town, take your fat bike or some skis. When we lived in a bush village, we often saw kids skiing to school from homes on the other side of the valley. When you have well-packed trails, these things can be done.

Figure 11: A fat bike for use on snow and ice.

Animal Power

Those first Alaskans that walked here didn't walk alone. They brought dogs. The dogs also carried things, whether on their backs or by dragging. Dogs are great for transport across snow. And you don't need an entire team to get some use out of man's best friend. Many people with a single dog will go skijoring (having a dog pull you while you are on skis). Our biggest dog will sometimes act as a freight dog, dragging sled loads of firewood. We also have a dog sled and a dog cart, and these can be used with only 2 or 3 dogs—if you want. You may not be competing in the Iditarod, but you can get some places a lot faster and a lot easier when dogs run with you and help with the load. Of course, having a full dog team can be great, but remember: you have to feed them.

Horses can be good transport in a lot of areas, but they're hard to use in winter. A lot of horse owners will even board their horses away from home during the winter. And whether you board horses or keep them at home, you still have an animal that you are feeding year-round, yet they can't live in the house with you as a cuddly pet and you can't get work out of them. They aren't very practical for an off-grid situation unless you can grow your own feed, and they are especially impractical for more remote settings.

It's hardly worth mentioning, but yaks can be good animal transport. There is a company that uses yaks for pack trips in the Alaska range. Because they are well-adapted to cold places, they might be a great year-round alternative to horse power. They're a bit expensive to buy, but they're good at feeding themselves (they browse like goats do). They can also provide milk and hair (see the "Food" chapter).

Figure 12: A dog team on the Iditarod Trail coming into a village checkpoint.

Current, Tide, and Wind Power

The forces of nature can move you pretty easily—when you're in a boat. Very few people are in a living situation in which they can use a boat as a main form of transportation, but those people are lucky. Some people live on sailboats, and some just use them to travel about. Some do both. For quite a while, Alaska's fishing fleet was mostly sail-powered—sailing can definitely be done up here. But to have a sailboat while living in an off-grid situation means that you have to have your own harbor, or at least a safe place to anchor your boat and a dinghy to get to shore. There are a few compatible places, but not many.

People that use boats for transportation in coastal areas can also use tides to their advantage. If you live somewhere in the Cook Inlet area, that means you travel north (up the inlet) as the tide comes in. You travel south (down the inlet) as the tide goes out. No gas necessary. With some of the most extreme tidal shifts in the world, you can let the tide do the work for you. Some people will even surf the bore tide that moves along Turnagain Arm. It might not be handy as a means of transportation, but it looks fun. And cold. Tides move in and out of bays and inlets all over the state. Make sure you know what you're doing before you try using tides to your advantage, though. And beware the shallows: many people will get bogged down in mudflats at low tide. Some stay stuck and drown. Don't be one of those.

River currents can also be handy. If you live along a navigable river, you'll find yourself traveling up or downriver all the time. It's a lot easier than cutting through the woods or across muskeg. Plus, the current does all the work for you when you're heading downstream. Traditionally, late winter and early spring was a time when certain groups of Alaska Natives would hike upriver to hunting or trapping camps. There they would hunt. And trap. And once the ice left the river, they would build a raft and float back down again for fishing season. They didn't even need to own a boat. Some people still use this strategy—hike upstream, raft downstream later. These days you can use an inflatable pack raft.

Gas Power

Automobiles

Do I need to tell you how to buy a car? No. Just buy one if you don't have one already. I think it would be amazing if you could get by without one, but difficult. If you plan to live on the road system, think about road maintenance. Think about the snowy times. The icy times. Four-wheel drive is a must. Studded tires are a must, and it's best to have a set of studded tires already on wheels—for quicker changeovers in fall and spring. Some people in more urban areas can get by with only front wheel drive, but that won't be you (unless you plan to only live off-grid seasonally, which some people do). And if you plan to live in a place you can drive a car to, will the road be plowed in winter? It probably won't. That's why we own a plow truck. We have about 3 miles of road to plow. Of course, with the recent warm winters, we only need it once or twice a year. But when you need it, you need it. Especially in case of emergency. And plow trucks themselves have their own quirks and requirements.

Some people shy away from diesel vehicles, as the fuel can turn jelly-like in very cold temperatures. If you plan to live in the Interior (i.e. Fairbanks, Delta Junction, Tok), you may want a block heater so you can plug in and get your engine warm enough to where it can start. Pickup trucks are the norm all over the state—they can transport firewood, building materials, moose carcasses, water containers, groceries, gas cans, propane tanks, and so on. SUVs and station wagons are also quite popular. You don't *have* to have a big vehicle. There's a lady around here that gets by with nothing more than a Geo Metro. It can be done.

4-wheelers

For many people in Alaska, the 4-wheeler (or ATV) is the primary form of transport (this includes many people already on the road system). If life rarely takes you out of your local area, you might not want to bother with a car. Of course, it is many people's vehicle of choice because they have too many DWIs to legally drive a regular vehicle. You're not supposed to drive drunk on ATVs, either, but it's a lot less likely that someone will get pulled over, unless they're very obvious and in a populated area.

ATVs are the vehicle of choice in most bush villages. It's hard to get full-sized cars and pickup trucks into villages that aren't on the road system. They have to be barged in, and that is expensive. But 4-wheelers can come in on planes. They're also extremely versatile, an attribute necessary for bush life. They can drive up and down steep slopes, through (and across) rivers and streams (not too deep, obviously), across muskeg, through mud, and on any packed trail during winter. With trailers, you can haul a variety of things. They may not be as warm and comfortable as passenger vehicles, but they are better adapted for local tasks in rural places.

Snowmachines

More commonly known (in the lower states) as snowmobiles, the snowmachine is essential to those in colder parts of the state. Most people can't wait for winter just so they can get riding again.

And they are a *lot* of fun to ride—not too great on gas mileage, so not necessarily practical in that sense, but they are practical in many other ways, mostly due to the nature of winter travel.

One freeze-up has happened and there is a good layer of snow, Alaska becomes a kind of playground. The things that used to keep people in one area (swamps, rivers, lakes, bays) are now as easy to cross as anything else—easier, in fact, as they won't have trees and stumps and downed logs to get in the way. And with a good-sized sled, a snowmachine can haul a lot more than a 4-wheeler can. That means firewood. Caribou. Building materials.

Many people who build in off-grid areas without road (or even trail) access will wait until winter and then use snowmachines to transport all of their building materials to their building site. This is a lot cheaper and more practical than having them flown in (especially if it's an area without suitable places to land). And it's still kind of fun.

Planes

If you can afford your own plane, you probably have a lot of money and don't need to read this book (no need to be practical). But if you live in certain areas, hiring local pilots might be the best thing. If you plan to stay in one area and only leave once or twice a year, having a bush pilot take you (and your gear) in and out is actually somewhat practical, especially if the terrain between you and civilization is not very friendly. You can also arrange to have occasional deliveries of food or other supplies.

There is a lot of Alaska that is "fly-in only." While that doesn't mean it would be impossible to get to these places overland, it does mean there aren't any trails good enough to make it feasible with any other vehicle.

Skiffs

Those living on rivers or lakes will probably want a skiff. Water travel is very efficient, and a lot of places you'll want to go are near water. I don't have much to say on the matter except this: pay attention to the keel and draught of your skiff. Different designs are better for different situations. If you're near a shallow river, you'll want a shallow draught and a flat keel. If you're on a large lake (one large enough to get choppy waves during wind), you'll want more draught and more keel.

There's one little trick worth mentioning, and it might not be new to you: wrap the cord (that has the killswitch) around your wrist, or attach it to yourself another way. That way if you're boating solo and something knocks you out of the boat (like an unexpected submerged log or a sandbar), the motor shuts off and your boat doesn't go too far. That and wear your life jacket. Seriously. The water is cold, even in summer.

You will learn how to detect different local dangers, both by listening to locals and by learning the way the water looks under normal conditions at different times of the year (so that you'll know when it looks out of the ordinary). It takes time to learn.

Getting Your Stuff Where it Needs to Go

We need to move much more than ourselves. We need building supplies. Appliances. Furniture. Food. There are a lot of ways to get your things to your site. When you live on the road system, it's easy: you drive to town, buy stuff, and bring it back in your vehicle. You may need a trailer for some things, but that's pretty standard. It all depends on where you live and what you need.

For building supplies, there are two main retailers: Home Depot and Spenard Builder's Supply, or "SBS" for short (both have several locations throughout the state). SBS does have a catalog that comes out regularly and has special deals for shipping things like home packages to bush locations—anywhere accessible by barge (most bush villages are either on the coast or on a navigable river, so barge schedules have been well-established for a very long time). Some towns will have local suppliers, local hardware stores, or even local mills (for lumber). Towns in Southeast Alaska also tend to get more deliveries by water, but the ships come up from Washington and shipping ends up being a lot cheaper for those in Southeast. Otherwise, big shipments come via the same cargo ships (but farther, having to stop in Southcentral Alaska for unloading/reloading, depending on whether things are being transferred to the road system or a ship/barge that will take them to bush villages in Western or Northern Alaska), or they might come via highway.

These ships are the same ones that people often utilize to move their household goods to Alaska. Many people will load up a shipping container, put it on a boat in Washington, and then meet it somewhere in Alaska. It ends up being a cheap and efficient option for a lot of people (relative to having to buy everything at Alaska prices). You can fit a lot of stuff in a shipping container. Once you've emptied it out (by moving things into your cabin), you'll have an excellent and durable storage shed.

For big items like automobiles, barges are the only way that they make it to locations off the road system. In some rare cases, an ice/snow road might make some places (closer to the road system) accessible to automobiles during winter when they would not be accessible in summer.

For medium-sized stuff (appliance-sized, or things like 4-wheelers and snowmachines), air cargo companies can bring it to the nearest airport (if you're off the road system), as well as those same barges. Otherwise, it's up to you to find a trailer, cargo sled, or skiff that will fit whatever your load is.

For everything smaller than that, we have mail order. That can be Amazon or it can be any other company that does shipping (though Amazon is most popular due to the higher likelihood of free shipping). If there is no parcel delivery service in your area (and there might not be), the boxes will just go to the post office and be waiting for you. If you live in the bush, few retailers will offer free shipping on anything. Try different ones and compare—put items in your "cart," then see what the shipping will be (but don't click the "buy" button just yet). When we lived in a bush village, I needed to order various outdoor goods. Cabela's is the popular choice, but I compared shipping costs and found that Sportsman's Guide always had cheaper shipping, so I went with them. It may or may not still be like that—I have no idea who has cheaper shipping these days. The point is simply to test it out so you can save as much money as possible.

Road and Trail Maintenance

There is a good chance that your road and/or trail will not be maintained by anybody but you and your neighbors. The state maintains bigger paved roads and highways. If you live in an organized borough, they will maintain most other main roads. If you have a city government, they might keep other city roads in shape. But if you're on the smaller side roads, there will probably not be public maintenance. The road that we live on is one such road, and we maintain most of the final 2-3 miles of this road. That's a lot of road.

Maintaining gravel roads and 4-wheeler trails is different from maintaining a footpath. With a footpath, you only need to keep it free of branches/brush and keep using it. Bigger trails (for 4-wheelers and snowmachines) don't require much maintenance. In winter, they need to be used regularly (whether by snowmachine or snowshoe) to stay nicely packed. They should not be plowed. In the warm season, they might get mucky and sticky—enough that ATVs can sink up to their axles. Particularly mucky areas can be improved by adding wooden planks (or branches) lengthwise along the existing ruts. Don't add loose dirt—that will just make things worse. Adding gravel is fine if you have access to it—the coarser, the better. Whatever you add to a mucky trail, you want to make sure it doesn't absorb or retain water. You want water to drain *through* it, not gather in it. If you can get a load of gravel to dump on a mucky area, it will last even longer if you put down some typar (road fabric) before putting the gravel in, though it won't be easy getting a roll of that stuff to a really remote area. The best long-term solution is to find ways to help the soil drain more quickly. If there are low areas where water gathers, try digging a small trench to let water flow into an even lower area (and away from your trail). Building your trail up in these lower areas is a good idea, but difficult work. You can't do it with mucky soil. You have to things like gravel, stones, and logs. The investment will be worth it if your trail is truly problematic. Nobody likes getting their 4-wheeler swamped.

I once helped a guy get his 4-wheeler (the side-by-side style) unstuck from a mucky section of a local trail. He was new—recently arrived from a lower state. But he had a nice new 4-wheeler with a winch, and he was sure it would be easy to get it unstuck, as he'd gotten easily unstuck from other places using this method. The only problem was that he didn't have enough cable on his winch to get to a big enough tree to use as an anchor to pull his vehicle out. So I walked back there with a tow strap, tied it around a tree, and then attached it to the hook on his winch. He started the winch and began gunning his engine. The engine raced but the 4-wheeler did not budge. Finally, the tow strap snapped. He couldn't believe it. His amazing winch and 4-wheeler had failed. I walked back home and got another tow strap. This time we tried a different tree. I asked if he needed help on the 4-wheeler end of things—maybe I could try driving it out of the muck for him. I thought he might let me, since he was an older guy and had some health problems. He said no. He knew what he was doing. Again, he started the winch and gunned his engine. The engine raced once more, even harder this time, the winch struggled, and the tow strap snapped. I started to get a little mad. I didn't have any more spare tow straps, so I went back and got a chain. We went through the process again. This time I stood right next to the 4-wheeler. He was getting ready to gun the engine again. I asked, "Are you sure you don't want me to help?" I offered to get a shovel, some boards, and a jack. He said no. He could handle it. I asked, "Are you sure it's in gear?" He looked. It wasn't. It was in neutral. It had been in neutral the *entire time*. He had never put it in gear at all. Once he put it in gear, the winch (combined with engine power) got it out easily. He was embarrassed, but I didn't say anything. He thanked me and I took my chain and went home.

Moral #1: always have a tow strap or two.

Moral #2: when a much more experienced person tries to give you advice about something, swallow your tough guy pride and listen.

Moral #3: don't drive unfamiliar trails in spring when the soil is mucky.

It can be awful: the top layers of soil have thawed, but the water (snowmelt combined with the water that was frozen in the soil) cannot drain anywhere because the soil underneath is still frozen. This means the top layers are almost like quicksand in some places. Again, knowing your local soil types and your local land (in general) is important. The guy came by my house the following week to drop off a load of moose meat as a way of saying "thank you." It wasn't exactly replacing the tow straps he needlessly broke, but it was appreciated.

If you do drive in mucky areas, you should (of course) have a tow strap handy, but you should also have a shovel, several boards (probably 6-8 pieces of various sizes—leftover scrap will probably do), and a jack. They'll get you unstuck when nothing else will. The process is simple:

1. Dig out (as much as possible) from around the affected tires.

2. Place a board on the ground where you plan to jack the vehicle up. It should be long and broad—perhaps a 2x8 or 2x10 scrap at least a couple of feet long. If there is not enough clearance beneath the vehicle to fit your jack and at least two boards, you'll need to do a little bit of digging here as well.
3. Place yet another board (slightly smaller) on top of this one. The idea is to not only give the jack a stable place to sit, but also to spread the weight of the vehicle out at much as possible over the greatest area. Since the soil is no doubt soft, you can't just put the jack directly on the ground. Trying to jack up a vehicle doing it that way will just push the jack into the ground. Use progressively smaller boards to build a mini-pyramid under the jack to spread the weight out.
4. Jack up the vehicle as much as possible.
5. Place your remaining boards beneath the affected tires. Dig out a little more if necessary.
6. Gently lower the vehicle down onto the boards, remove the jack, and put the jack and jack support boards away.
7. Drive away.

I once got a panicked call from a neighbor. He wanted me to pull his truck out of a mucky spot where it had gone off the road. Other neighbors had tried to pull him out and failed, but he knew my plow truck could handle it. It had pulled him out of a winter drift before (his was a large truck—long bed, 4 full-sized doors, 7.3 liter engine…you can probably figure out the model). I told him I'd love to help but I was out of town—and across a body of water. Not on the road system at the moment. But I asked him if he had a shovel, scrap boards, and a jack. He said he did. I described the process in detail. He paused. Thought. He said, "Well, I guess I'll have to get dirty then." But he never did. He just kept calling people until somebody with a strong enough vehicle agreed to bail him out. He could have done it himself in about an hour. He had the wrong attitude. You can't move out here and expect people to bail you out all the time. You need to learn to do things for yourself. He didn't just *not* learn. He refused to learn. And he moved away about 5 months later.

Maintaining a gravel road is a little simpler than maintaining off-road trails, mainly because you can drive on it and easily deliver material. Most of the time it will be gravel. We patch a lot of potholes on our road. If the potholes are really deep, we put large beach rocks down on the bottom of them, then we pack smaller rocks in the spaces between those, then dump basic "pit run" gravel on top to cement it all together. Patched potholes should be slightly higher than the road around them, as they will compact over time as they are driven on more and more (eventually evening out). If an entire section of road is mucky or worn down, you may want to put a piece of road fabric down first. Road fabric is tremendously important in keeping roads from getting too soggy. There is another newcomer in the area that tries to help maintain the road by patching potholes, but he does it in a way that wastes his time and does not benefit the road. He adds sawdust. He puts spruce branches in potholes. He uses material that absorbs water or gets blown by the wind. I even told him once, in a very straightforward manner: nobody that lives on this road wants anything added to the road unless it is sand or gravel. He continued adding sawdust.

You can't fix stupid.

Speaking of winter, maintenance in winter consists of two things: sanding and plowing. If things get icy, add sand. Get it from the beach or from a supplier (usually gravel suppliers will also have sand). It will improve traction and it will also help ice melt faster. This year, I placed a series of buckets (full of sand) by the side of the road in the area most prone to icy danger. They will be there when we need them. They've already been used once on a particularly icy day when two different neighbors went off the road in that same spot. Then they disappeared for a few days. I called around. "Where are my buckets?" I asked. Nobody had them—they must have gone with the one neighbor I didn't call. And they were back later that day—full of sand. Nobody had to tell him to do that. He just knew.

Plowing is a little trickier than sanding. It's actually an art in some ways. I won't get into the finer points, but there are some important things to remember when plowing a road:

- Go fast enough that the plow throws the snow well off of the road (keep your plow blade angled so the snow flies in the right direction). You want to keep the snow as far from the road as possible.

- Keep your plow along the very edge of the road—or even hanging slightly off the road, if possible. Again, keep the driving surface as wide as possible and don't let the berm encroach. As winter progresses, the berm will have no choice but to come in slightly each time. You want to postpone that for as long as possible. Sometimes it will come in so far that the road becomes too narrow to get through. That would be bad.
- If there are any unused driveways or pull-out areas, pile snow there. Leave spaces for cars to pull out and let others pass (these will be essential later in winter, as the road *will* get narrower and vehicles will need places to pass each other).
- Pile snow in places that will be convenient in spring. Think about the direction that water will run off when the piles melt. If the snow begins to melt and water runs across the road, this will refreeze during cool spring nights, creating extra ice on the road. Putting it on the downhill side of the road whenever possible is the way to go.
- If there is an area where snow commonly drifts over the road, you'll want to plow it regularly and keep it pushed back. These are the areas that are likely to cause the biggest problems, as the drifts will shrink the width of the road faster than regular snowfall will. Consider adding snow fencing to prevent drifting in vulnerable areas. The fences should be set well back from the road (100 feet or so), as snow blows over a snow fence and settles on the leeward (*not* the windward) side. You want to give it space to settle on the leeward side of the fence before it gets to the road.

I rarely bother plowing unless it has snowed 6 inches or more. If it is less than 6 inches, I'd rather just drive on it and pack it down. This works very well if you can get your neighbors to do it, too. Unfortunately, people have a habit of following each other's tracks in fresh snow. Make a point to always drive on the highest part of the road. That way you won't have to plow as often—it will be evenly packed down to each edge. Think of *every* vehicle as a road maintenance vehicle. Whether the road is snowy or not, making ruts is bad. When people constantly drive in the same tracks, it will only make things worse—especially when the road is soft in spring and fall. All gravel roads wear down over time, but wearing down evenly is the best way to go.

Figure 13: A rutted 4-wheeler trail in dry conditions.

Time and Teamwork

It's easy to get used to being able to go anywhere at any time at (just about) any speed. And it's a lovely thing: to be able to just hop in your car and drive when you feel like it (assuming the traffic cooperates). Getting used to a different speed of life can be difficult. It might even be impossible for some. You have to be okay with certain things taking a LOT longer than you are used to.

Take heating your home, for example. You are probably used to having a thermostat on a wall somewhere. You set the thermostat to the desired temperature and then forget about it. That didn't take long, did it? But just the act of brining in firewood, building a fire, and maintaining it might take up an hour of your day or more (once all the time is added up). And that's not even counting the time it takes to get the firewood.

I was thinking about this earlier today as I got ready to drive to work. I started the vehicle and turned the defroster on. I had to brush several inches of snow off of the vehicle. Once the loose snow was gone, I noticed that there was still pebbled ice on everything—and a lot of snow was sticking to that ice. That's because we had a brief round of freezing rain yesterday, then snowfall. No problem. Just a few extra minutes of defrosting.

I drove down the road as a reasonable speed. There was enough snow to make it a little bit slidey, but nothing I'm not used to. As usual, I drove as far over as I could, trying to widen the road with the tires (widening the road by chipping away at the snow berm at the road's edge). Sometimes the snow would try to suck me over the edge and into the ditch, but I resisted. I left our unmaintained road by turning onto a borough-maintained road. It still had not been plowed, so I took it slow and kept it in 4-wheel drive. When I got to the end and was ready to turn on the paved, state-maintained road, I took it out of 4-wheel drive. This was a little bit premature, as my tires were still on soft snow and they were spinning, trying to get traction. I eased off the gas and tried again, but more slowly. The tires got traction and worked fine. I just had to accelerate slowly. No big deal. There was nobody coming down the road. I wasn't holding anyone else up. I wasn't even going to be late for work. I planned plenty of time for my drive.

We also have to take time out of our day for shoveling. My wife saved me a lot of time today by plowing the road. I tend to be the one that does the plowing, but she's also quite good at it. Our teamwork is essential to our success. I already noted that she does most of the firewood cutting, transporting, splitting, and stacking. I do most of the building. She does most of the gardening. I work the wage job so we'll have money for food. She cooks more often, but I do breakfast most days. I could go on and on, but the point is clear—there's a lot to be done, especially when you have young kids.

You can never be in a hurry. In winter, heating bath water might take an hour. You won't be getting pizza deliveries or cooking meals in a microwave—another hour of your day will be dedicated to food preparation. Driving to town for groceries (technically about 24 miles) might take an hour. You might be trying to drive somewhere but traffic is stopped for moose on the road. If it's a small road, you might have to wait while neighbors talk. If you don't have your own plow, you might have to wait for someone to come and do the plowing for you. You can't be hasty trying to get your vehicle unstuck—if you just push on the gas pedal harder, you'll only get stuck worse.

If you have no choice but to be spending so much of your time simply existing, then why live here at all? It's simple: you have to enjoy those things that take up that time. I enjoy plowing the road. My wife enjoys cooking (and I enjoy eating). We both enjoy chopping wood. Sometimes things get redundant, but you can sing while you work. You can turn work into a game. People have been doing this forever. There will always be monotonous tasks. Neither of us really enjoy shoveling snow, but it becomes fun when you try throwing the snow at different targets—like one of the dogs. Then they shake it off and get excited and jump around a bit.

I ordered a book from Amazon 26 days ago. It still hasn't arrived.

We once had neighbors that always drove in a hurry. Our road is not compatible with hurried drivers. The potholes will vibrate anything loose that can be loosened. We would collect pieces of their truck as we drove down the road. Hose clamps. The piece of plastic bearing the truck's model number. License plate. Eventually the truck tried to take a turn too quickly and ended up stuck in a ditch for three weeks (this wasn't the first time it had gone in a ditch—it had done once before in winter, but I pulled it out, and once that spring, when he refused to dig it out and found someone else to extract it).

When your truck is in the ditch for three weeks, you are no longer in a hurry. Problem solved.

Anecdote: Learning Off-Grid on an Alaskan Lake

Between our time living in a remote bush village and the year we spent in Southeast Alaska, my wife and I worked for a summer as backcountry rangers on a semi-accessible Alaskan lake. It wasn't terribly remote—you could walk several miles of trail to get to it—but the hike was inconvenient enough that a lot of visitors preferred to take float planes when visiting the lake. It seemed like the distance from the road would weed out any lazy or irresponsible visitors, but we were wrong. A single short summer would teach us a lot about transportation and human nature.

The summer itself was a particularly wet and buggy one. It rained. A lot. We spent far too much time indoors, playing solitaire, listening to the radio, or reading. I read a 1000-page novel in less than a week. It was *that* rainy. And the bugs! Mosquitoes are bad around inland bodies of water, but they were so bad on the lake that summer that we couldn't escape them by staying indoors. They were resourceful. They'd find the crevices. They'd sneak in. We ended up buying a large mosquito net and draping it over our bed. Otherwise we would not have been able to sleep. Nothing keeps you from relaxing like the recurring buzz of a mosquito hovering around your head. The buzzing stops and you wonder: did it go away? Is it biting me right now? You start slapping yourself in the head and neck just in case. That's no way to get to sleep.

If we were working outside, we'd wear thin, long-sleeved gear and hats to keep our skin covered but not too hot. And we would perpetually keep a fire going in the front yard of the cabin, maybe 25 or 30 feet from the lake's edge. That's when we learned a lesson in laziness. Even though our cabin was clearly labeled as the ranger's cabin and even though our firewood was clearly a private supply for *our* use only, it would disappear at times. Lazy campers from nearby campsites would take it while we were out patrolling the lake. They had neglected to bring their own, and they were too lazy to find their own (they weren't allowed to cut living trees, but that would have resulted in green wood that wouldn't be good for fires anyway). Even though it was clearly noted (perhaps even widely publicized) that visitors needed to bring their own firewood, theft happened at least once every couple of weeks. And people would *still* cut small trees for firewood. There's something about being out in nature that causes a certain type of person—men who feel the need to prove their masculinity—to ignore any park rules that might get in the way of their display of manliness. They'd cut down a tree, dammit, because that's what guys do when they're camping.

Our duties were simple. We needed to: keep the trail to the lake maintained, keep the public cabins (four of them were on the lake) clean and maintained, contact any campers that needed to be reminded of the rules, help any campers that needed help, and give occasional radio reports back to headquarters. There were other specialized duties that would pop up from time to time, like digging a new outhouse hole for an outhouse that needed to be moved. The main thing, though, was to keep those cabins in good shape for whichever visitors were coming next. But the cabins were not easy to get to—they were at various locations around the lake, which meant we needed to boat all over the place on a daily basis. And the motor for the skiff was out of order—it wouldn't be fixed until the middle of summer, or so we were told. That left us with a canoe as our only way of getting around the lake.

Neither of us had used a canoe before. It felt a bit topply at first, but it didn't take very long to get the hang of it. Within a couple of days we were able to get anywhere we needed to go, as fast as the canoe could take us. We became experts at landing and launching. We even started to enjoy it—there's something to be said for gliding across the lake without all the extra noise of an outboard motor. Sometimes we would have to battle winds and whatever waves could be whipped up on that lake—it *could* be challenging. But usually the water was peaceful. We would sometimes just let ourselves float for a while—really get out into the middle of the water so we could see beyond the tops of the trees to the distant mountains. Using the canoe also allowed us to get closer to the wildlife that frequented the lake. Loons were very common, and we cherished their calls. We hadn't really been around loons before. They're magical creatures. There were also resident beavers. We could tell where they'd been eating—there were tell-tale tree stumps along the shoreline in certain areas, short with a pointed cone at top, little grooves where teeth had gnawed straight through the birches. We even saw three moose swimming across the lake one afternoon. And they saw us, hurrying to a run once they reached land. People in a canoe must look scary to them.

The human wildlife was surprisingly…wild. They normally would have been quite tame. They were city dwellers. Townies. People that didn't camp very often—which is why they liked having clean cabins ready for them at a lake they could fly into. The ones that hiked in would always overestimate their strength and stamina. They would carry in all kinds of things and then decide they didn't want to carry them back out again, even though they were supposed to pack everything back out (including their trash). The cabins were a place they could get away from it all. A place they could get crazy and forget how much they hated their lives. A place where they could clear their heads (or makes their heads particularly foggy with booze). A place to reset their clocks and breathe clean air and hear nothing but the loons and gentle lake waves. There didn't seem to be any in-between: visitors were either looking for a place to party or they were seeking serenity. The partiers definitely outnumbered the quiet ones.

The main thing they would leave behind was trash. We hauled 40-50 pounds of trash out of there on a weekly basis. They would also leave food behind. Sometimes that was a welcome treat for us. Once we found a big plastic sack full of unopened beer cans sitting in shallow water by the shore—just chilling in the lake water, literally. The sack had been forgotten. *We* didn't forget it. We took it back to our cabin and made it last. Some people left behind tools—they would bring saws and things like that. One group left behind a brand-new air mattress. A really nice one. They hauled it in and didn't realize how heavy it was. They didn't want to take it back out, so they left it. Sometimes they'd leave behind little stumps where they just had to show off and cut a tree down. There were multiple groups that left behind big piles of poop. One time it was just sitting right in the middle of a trail. Another time it was right next to one of the outhouses. It was perplexing: why not just go in the outhouse? Maybe they were leaving it as a gift for us.

Some people actually did leave gifts—legitimate ones, not turds. They'd be small gifts—little treats or something. These would be from the people that made a serious effort to clean their own camp. We kept track, and it seemed like the ratio of responsible campers to irresponsible campers was about 1 to 5—not a very good ratio. Does that mean most people are selfish slobs? It probably does. It's something I think about far too often, but that job showed us just what people are like when they're out in the wilds and they don't think anyone is watching.

They trash it.

A lot of Alaskans talk about how little of our state is actually owned by the state and its citizens, and how much is owned by the federal government. It's usually in the form of a complaint—the idea is that we should own more of our state and have better access to its resources. There is a lot of merit to the argument, especially when ownership is compared to that seen in other states. On the other hand, a lot of the federally owned land is inaccessible or incredibly unique and very profitable for tourism (i.e. Denali), generating far more money with tourism than it ever could by resource extraction. I would like to think that, should the federal government ever give up control of its lands here (i.e. National Parks, Forests, and Monuments, BLM land, etc.), Alaskans would be responsible and care for them—using them, but doing it responsibly. But from what I have seen, I am skeptical. I imagine that places—especially places you can drive to—would get trashed, forests would be cut, and wildlife would disappear rapidly. That's already true of most places you can drive to that *aren't* protected. If only those people that live in these rural areas had access to the resources, they might last. Locals would better understand the importance of keeping enough resources (like trees and wildlife) alive so that future generations of those resources can continue providing for us. But if they are open to the hundreds of thousands of others in the cities, they surely will not last. In times past, these issues would probably be resolved with violence: outsiders coming in to an area to take your resources would not be welcome, especially if they are resources your local community depends on. But we're all Americans. It doesn't work like that. We can't legally keep people from driving here from Anchorage and taking local animals, trees, and fish. We may grumble and complain about the feds owning much of our state, but if they didn't, we'd be grumbling and complaining about the city dwellers that come to our neighborhoods, take what they want, and leave nothing but trash. I'm not sure who I'd rather complain about. Probably both. I think I am already doing that.

The second half of our summer was different. The skiff motor was fixed and we started to use the skiff to dart around the lake. We could make our rounds much more quickly, of course. Since we had to beach the skiff (there were no docks at the cabins we maintained), we always had to be sure to pull the motor up as we got shallower, but that was the only thing tricky about it. With gasoline power, we were able to cover a lot more ground. Except it wasn't ground. It was water. It was easier to go to the more remote corners of the lake. It wasn't tiring. So it was nice—but a different kind of nice. Ultimately, I think we both preferred the canoe. Given enough time, we would have taken that canoe to every corner of the lake as well. But that's how it goes when motors get involved: you no longer have enough time. You're always going faster and farther and doing more. The time you save by going faster is rarely used for anything meaningful. In the cities and suburbs, we spend all afternoon driving around, running errands, getting so much accomplished—things that would have taken days or even weeks in generations past. Those saved days and weeks? Spent at work, making somebody else richer (usually). Spent at home, watching TV (also making somebody else richer). Working to be a consumer. And those hours on the lake that we saved by using the motor? Spent back at the cabin, probably, playing cards and reading books. Those hours on the lake would have been better spent in the canoe, getting to know every inch of shoreline in detail. Getting to know the beaver houses. Listening to the loon calls. The hours we save by running errands in our vehicles? Who knows what we could do with them if they weren't spent being more efficient consumers. Maybe we could be building something. Getting to know our neighbors. Going somewhere at human speed. Stopping to smell the roses and all that.

Stopping to swat the mosquitoes.

Chapter Nine: Entertainment

Those planning an off-grid future in Alaska don't often think about how they'll entertain themselves. More than likely, the general plan is to be so busy with trying to survive that entertainment won't be needed—there will always be wood to chop, fish to catch, and so on. But that isn't really the case. Something *else* is needed, especially in winter months when light is limited and your batteries are running low. It's possible to stay so occupied during summer and fall that there just isn't time for hobbies—that's true for most of us. But winter generally lasts from November thru April (longer for some areas). It can be maddening because it will seem like spring is coming at least once—there will be a warm spell—and then *second* winter hits. Sometimes there's even a third winter. Cabin fever is real, and I've known people that have legitimately gone crazy from it. They may not have been officially diagnosed as crazy, but I could tell they weren't quite right.

Reading

You know how to read. You might even be one of those that truly enjoys it. You like it enough to buy a book like this from some random yokel on the internet. That's a good sign. You probably like other books as well. I recommend three types of books in particular:

- Nonfiction Alaskana: books about local plants, traditional Native practices, history, how-to-do things the Alaskan way, and so on. You're reading one now, but there are others. Some are very specific and very useful. Some are just fun. All are good to have on your shelf. At the very least, they tell you this: people can and do thrive in Alaska. That's a good thing to remember in the middle of winter when you've just about had enough.
- Humor: because you'll want to laugh regularly.

- Novels: being mentally transported to (and immersed in) other worlds and settings is a good thing for your brain (books do this a lot better than movies do). It keeps your mind off of stressors. It relieves the sometimes monotonous weather. Plus, they're just enjoyable. You'll have so much time to read that people will be impressed with how well-read you have become. Big classics like *War and Peace*? Pssh. Those are nothing.

Music

There isn't a human alive that doesn't love music. It is part of who we are. We've always made music. We've always loved listening to it. Most of us even move to it from time to time.

As I type this, my older daughter is reading on the couch adjacent to my chair. Our infant daughter is playing with toys on the floor. My wife is playing guitar in the next room. We are all listening as we go about our morning. It is December 14. It is 15 degrees out and the wind is 10 miles per hour. A little bit of wind noise, but not much. The fire is going and I just poured fresh coffee. We make an effort to play music every day, even though the conditions are not always ideal (and it's not so easy when you have school, work, kids, and the like). Music is that important to our mental health. And when you live in a situation when you can't just switch on a stereo, playing your own is sometimes the best way to hear your favorite songs.

While you will still be able to listen to music in your off-grid home, just remember that power might be limited in winter months. Even if you're just playing music from your phone or laptop, those batteries will still need to be charged. You can make your own music without needing any electricity at all. You can even do it in the dark if you want. And I'm not making a lewd joke. And I'm not talking about one of those hand-crank phonographs, either. I just mean making it on instruments.

The kinds of instruments available to you will depend on your living situation. Guitars are a good choice anywhere, and it's easy to get a "travel size" guitar. Mandolins, banjos, violins, mountain dulcimers, and ukuleles are also quite portable. If you're a keyboard player moving somewhere remote, consider taking up accordion (the left hand buttons aren't that tricky to figure out—each button is a different chord, and they're patterned on the circle of fifths). We have road access, so we have a piano (getting it here was still pretty rough, and I had to buy a piano tuning kit to tune it afterward). Your home could be full of music. And if you don't play an instrument now, you'll have time to learn.

In times past, winter was always full of song and dance—especially in Alaska, whether in Native communities or in communities of outside settlers. Dancing helps you stay warm. Music makes you feel happy and, when you do it with others, it makes you feel connected. It's easy to feel *dis*connected in this day and age. People spend more time looking at phones and less time looking at each other. We may still be communicating, but it isn't the same. Lack of connection leads to a decline in mental health. Living in remote or off-grid places puts you at a further disadvantage for feeling connected, so I highly recommend finding people to play, sing, and dance with. If you're a churchgoing person, that can be easy (if you can make it to a church and if it happens to be the type that has music…not many have dancing). If you aren't, then you should make an effort to find out where people are playing music and go there, even if you aren't going to be playing yourself. It's good for you.

Winter in off-grid Alaska is the perfect time to master an old instrument or learn a new one. Put it on your list.

The Glowing Screen

Here I was just trash talking phones (and the other devices that connect us and disconnect us, depending on how we use them) and I have the nerve to bring them up as a source of entertainment. If you have enough power to keep phones and laptops charged (or to even run a full-sized desktop computer), then these can still be valuable tools *and* be entertainment. How versatile!

Even when not connected to Internet, devices already serve a lot of purposes—you can use them for reading, for music, for writing, for photos, for watching movies or shows, and so on (I also use my laptop for recording music, though that isn't as common). With the advent of streaming services, not as many laptops are coming with DVD drives. That's great for people who live *on* the grid and have access to reliable high-speed internet. For those of us that don't want to have our internet turned on all the time (which means we have to have our inverter running for the modem and router to work), that's *not* so great. We choose to use our laptop to watch DVDs for exactly that reason: we can enjoy shows or movies without having to turn the inverter on.

Streaming is not a good option for most in off-grid Alaska—yet. While many areas don't have good options for internet, our area does, and we could (if we wanted) use it for streaming. It's fast enough. We'll stream videos from time to time, and the speed is definitely sufficient. We just don't want to be plugged in 24/7. What's nice about our method is that DVDs are "on their way out," so they can be bought cheaply (or we just borrow them from one of the local libraries).

If it's possible to have internet capable of streaming, then it's possible to have satellite TV as well. In fact, some of our neighbors just down the hill have it. But that runs into the same issues you find when you have your internet running all the time: you have to use more energy, and you'll find that it's easy to forget that Alaska is just outside your door. It's hard to know when a person has crossed over from controlling these tools to being controlled by them.

Gatherings

Just because you're planning on moving away from as many people as possible doesn't mean you hate people. No, you love people. *Your* people. Chances are good that other people that want to live in a similar situation might end up having a lot in common with you. They might just be your kind of people. If you aren't careful, you might end up making friends with your neighbors. At the very least, you'll find that most people in rural Alaska are friendly and helpful. There are a few that are a little bit crazy as well, but that's to be expected. They probably think you're a little bit crazy, too.

That bit of insanity is actually the hallmark of several of Alaska's most popular gatherings. We gather to do crazy things because we're all a little crazy, but secretly we're doing it so we don't end up going *really* crazy. Makes sense, right?

Take 4th of July, for example. Usually Americans get their crazy out by lighting off a bunch of fireworks and getting really drunk and possibly lighting themselves on fire either from too much lighter fluid on the grill or those same fireworks. At the very least, one can expect to either pelt or be pelted by a roman candle. But we don't really do 4th of July fireworks in Alaska. Some people will go to Houston (just about the only place in Alaska where you can buy them) and get a personal supply, but most of us don't want to start wildfires. And it doesn't get dark enough at night to have a regular fireworks show. So we find other ways to celebrate. Many towns have a nice little parade. But Seward holds a big race where people run to the top of a very steep mountain and then run back down. And it's *very* steep. Some people tumble down and get themselves cut up on the rocky scree. You'll usually see a lot of bloody people coming down Mt. Marathon on the 4th of July. A few years back, a guy went up and never came down. He just disappeared. They still haven't found him (and they looked pretty hard). It's serious business. In the "town" of Glacier View, 4th of July is celebrated by launching a series of cars from the top of a local cliff. They fly, crash, and become wreckage. The crowd at the bottom (a safe distance away) cheers. They measure for distance and keep records. This is also serious business.

Summer also features regional fairs and music festivals all over the state. Probably the most well-known are Salmonfest in August (in Ninilchik) and the state fair in late August/early September (in Palmer). There are baseball games, including the famous "midnight sun" baseball game in Fairbanks (in case you ever wanted to watch a baseball game at midnight).

There are fewer large events in fall. Most people are too busy getting the last of the preparations in place for winter, though some places celebrate the end of summer. Homer, for example, does a gathering in which they create a big, fancy wicker basket—a work of art, really—and then they light it on fire. It's a ritual, and there are similar small celebrations in various places, but things quiet down and gatherings go local until the new year.

Once winter has been around for a few months, people recognize the importance of getting together again. It isn't that winter is cold. It's the *length* of winter that makes it hard—not just for heating, but for mental and emotional health. So when we get halfway in, we need to do some things to reconnect with our fellow humans. One big event is known as "Fur Rondy" (formerly "Fur Rendezvous"), which is a holdover from territorial days. It started like similar rendezvous celebrations in the mountain states downstates—trappers gathering at a specified time and place to have fun, sell goods, gossip, and generally bask in humanity for a while. The modern Rondy is more like a two-week fair or festival—games, demonstrations, music, vendors, and even some sled dog races.

Speaking of sled dog races, they're another popular winter activity. Each region (apart from Southeast Alaska) has at least one long distance race. Southwest Alaska has the Kuskokwim 300. The Kenai Peninsula has the Tustumena 200 (though it has been cancelled several times in recent years due to lack of snow). Mat-Su has the Knik 200 (which has also had some recent cancellations due to lack of snow), the Willow 300, and the Northern Lights 300. The Copper River Valley has the Copper River 300. The eastern Interior (Fairbanks to the Canadian border) has the Yukon Quest—an annual 1000-mile race that usually has the harshest conditions of all. That race doesn't actually end at the Canadian border—it runs from Fairbanks to Dawson City, Yukon (or it goes from Dawson City to Fairbanks—it switches off every year). Northwest Alaska has the Kobuk 440. The big one—the Iditarod—starts in Willow and goes through the Alaska Range and the western Interior before reaching the Bering Sea coast, finally ending in Nome. It used to start in Anchorage, but the snow between Anchorage and Willow is no longer predictable. There's still a ceremonial start in Anchorage—itself a giant party—before the restart happens in Willow, which itself is another big event (though the restart has been moved from Willow to Fairbanks twice in recent years, also due to lack of snow). And the race remains a big deal for every single stop along the way, all the way until Nome. Iditarod is a mid-winter break for every checkpoint village. Something different. New people in town. A little bit of tourist money. The timing of the race—March—also has significance. It's when light is coming back enough to really lift a person's spirits. Spring is just around the corner (after a bit of second winter, of course).

Spring gatherings get a little bit crazy again. People are sick of winter. The temperatures are warming but there's still snow. There's a big festival in the mountains above Valdez called "Tailgate." Things are melting elsewhere, but there's still enough snow in the mountains for a big snowboard festival, but it's not limited to that—there's snowmachining and a general BBQ-and-party kind of atmosphere. During Girdwood's spring carnival, there's an event called the "slush cup" in which skiers and snowboarders dress in bizarre costumes (often ensembles like shorts-with-a-cape) and take turns racing down a hill and attempting to jump over a giant pond of slushy water at the bottom. Few make it across the pond and most end up getting very wet and cold and not caring a whole lot about it. It's part of the fun. Many are also drunk, so there's that.

Gatherings at the local level are different no matter what time of year. Most live music takes place in bars, and it happens regularly—so there's often a place to go to hear music if you happen to be in or near a town. Bigger towns will get touring acts and various kinds of performances. There are always small craft fairs and various festivals—you'd be surprised at the number of people that do things like wood carving, wool-spinning, quilting, ivory carving (Alaska Natives only for ivory work, unless it is "fossil," or pre-1972 ivory), painting, sculpting, pottery, poetry, and so on. People gather at church events or at neighbor's houses—local gatherings mostly resemble the kind of thing you'd expect to see in any "frontier" kind of place (except we don't really have traveling snake-oil salesmen putting on a show and we don't have public hangings…otherwise, it's a lot like watching a western).

The smaller the town, the more important that sporting events are. There used to be a minor-league hockey team in Anchorage, but no longer. And while Sarah Palin made it seem like hockey is the popular sport in Alaska (by being a "hockey mom"), basketball is *far* more popular, especially in villages. Almost every village has a school, and that usually means a gym. And any school with enough students is going to have a basketball team. Community basketball games are a big deal. They're often crowded, full of people of all ages (even if they aren't related to anyone in the team). Most village schools have a policy of opening the school gym to the public on a regular basis (even daily). Since a lot of villages have very few large buildings, having a heated, well-lit, large place in which everyone is welcome means that the school gym is the gathering place for anyone and everyone. You'll even find senior citizens down on the court playing ball, and many local tournaments will even have a special bracket for them. Even when a village team is playing an away game, you'll often find a crowd of people at the school watching the game together via internet (another thing about village schools is that they usually have the best internet in town; these viewing parties will also happen with volleyball and wrestling, which are also popular). Basketball is still a "thing" in bigger towns and cities, and college teams do enjoy popularity in places like Anchorage, but it does not have the central importance to the community that it does in the very small towns.

Speaking of Anchorage, it's a place people go for almost any reason. Some people like to go shopping at Costco. Some like to go to the indoor water park. Many coming from dry villages (where it is illegal to import, possess, or manufacture alcoholic beverages) like the opportunity to have a drink. There are movie theaters. Shopping malls. Restaurants. Sometimes people will just go to Anchorage because it's something to do. It's where most of the people are. Don't be surprised if you find yourself driving to Anchorage in the middle of the winter *just because*. A lot of people do that.

Anecdote: Learning Off-Grid in a Village

If you paid attentions to the earlier anecdotes, you'll know that we moved to a remote village not long after arriving in Alaska—just after spending a couple of months in Anchorage and then a failed attempt at spending the summer camping on the first lot we owned. Village life is different from road system life. It's also different from wilderness life. And each village is different from the next. We moved out to the west coast, 400+ miles from the road system.

It wasn't *technically* off-grid. The village had its own little power plant and mini-grid. Every village that's inhabited year-round does. It also had plumbing. Not every village has plumbing. Many have a central watering point and people haul water to their homes on a daily basis. In those villages, they poop in "honeybuckets" and have the buckets picked up and then deposited in the sewage lagoon or treatment plant. In this sense, we were lucky compared to many people who live in bush villages. It's possible to live very comfortably in the villages without plumbing—it just would have been that much harder to adjust to our new surroundings. There was plenty to get used to without having to worry about hauling water and making sure our poop got picked up.

Anecdote within an anecdote: the preschool teacher told us a story about a little boy who sometimes lived in our village and sometimes lived with family in a different village—one without plumbing. When she asked him which place he liked better, he said he liked our village better. When she asked why, his answer was simple: "Here we don't keep our poop."

In our two years in the village, we learned a lot. Much of it is documented in the upcoming book *A Kass'aq Comes and Goes*. In regards to off-grid living, there were some recurring themes, mostly having to do with "doing without" or "making due." Village life requires constant adaptation because the degree of isolation means that links to the outside world (and the luxuries of industrialized civilization) are tenuous. There are villages that have run out of gas toward the end of winter, requiring emergency deliveries at great cost. Without gas, the 4-wheelers and snowmachines don't go. Hunts don't happen. People don't eat. That didn't happen to us, but we experienced a variety of other disruptions.

One of the first disruptions was an issue getting food. We brought as much as possible in our packs—fresh stuff, mostly, since we had heard that getting good fruit and vegetables in the village was difficult. What you will find at a typical village store is usually older than what you'd find in most stores (since it takes longer to get there) and a lot more expensive (since shipping is expensive, especially for products that need to be refrigerated). We had ordered groceries from one of the stores in Anchorage that was supposed to do bush orders. These orders were *supposed* to arrive promptly—promptly enough that it was reasonable to order perishable goods. But the order didn't arrive. Days passed. We kept calling the store. We kept calling the airlines (almost everything comes in on planes). A neighbor gave us a bag of crowberries to help out with our fresh food situation. Finally the order came, roughly a week late. Much was rotten. The yogurt had gone bad. So had the milk. And the cheese. Bananas were smashed. The box had sat at the regional hub airport for days, ignored, forgotten. It had not been handled with care. It had not been kept in a refrigerated area.

We learned not to trust airlines to handle anything with care (which we already kind of knew, having seen some of the baggage handlers in Anchorage). We found other ways of keeping a balanced diet without depending on regular and expensive deliveries. We picked berries—20 gallons or so by the time berry season was over. These would last us through winter. Meat was also prohibitively expensive at the store, so we would go fishing. I would hunt what I could hunt on foot (snowshoe hares and spruce grouse). My wife became an expert at cooking hare, and we had it every way imaginable. We didn't enjoy powdered milk, but it became our mainstay. We fancied it up, though. We drank hot chocolate regularly. My wife bought yogurt starter and we made our own yogurt using the powdered milk. We picked dandelion greens for salads. And anytime I had to go to Anchorage (i.e. for a conference or training), I made sure to bring back as much fresh food as possible—and I wouldn't trust it to the baggage handlers. It went carry-on.

One such trip to Anchorage (a field trip with several students, actually) got me back to the regional airport at about the same time that a big storm came in. The airlines were refusing to fly, but the school district plane was actually there (yes, the school district had its own plane, a 16-seater, and we were lucky to have it there at the time, as it was usually in a different town). Our district pilot agreed to try getting us to our respective villages. Landing in village #1 was just about the scariest thing I've ever experienced. The snow was thick to the point that there was next to no visibility. He was flying by instrument, for the most part (using his radar/GPS gear). When he came down to the airstrip, the plane was gliding nearly sideways, facing into the fierce wind. He corrected at the last second to get the plane safely onto the ground. Village #2 was to be my village. He circled the airstrip several times but had to give up. He didn't think it was possible. I was a little bit mad—it seemed like he was a good enough pilot to make it happen. And I hadn't seen my wife in a week. I wanted to go home. But I accepted his decision. I wanted to live more than I wanted to get home.

There was another village or two to stop at. I wouldn't be the only one that wasn't getting home on time. So we made it back to the town where the plane normally stayed—where the school district headquarters could be found. We were taken in, fed, given places to stay. These things happen far too often for anyone to think twice about helping stranded travelers. The following day, the pilot was supposed to be taking different school board members back to their home villages. There was enough room for myself and the two students from my village to go on the plane as well. We would be dropped off. I got a little bit mad again when the pilot flew right over our village to go on to another one. "What the hell?" I thought. "He could have just dropped us off right now!" I was very eager to get home. But there were elders on the plane, and elders *always* go first. After accepting the situation and checking my ego, I enjoyed the trip, getting to see the entire region, including villages I never thought I'd go to. Had the weather been a little less cloudy, I would have seen Russia—we did fly right along the Bering Strait at one point.

This is where we learned that you should never be in a hurry about *anything*. Sometimes the power would go out. We could have complained and called up whoever is in charge of maintaining the power plant. But there would be no point. It would be fixed when it could be fixed. We'd just bundle up and assume the heat would come back on when it came back on (the teacher housing building, which had been the old elementary school, had a boiler in the basement that was responsible for the heat, and it required power to run). Sometimes the water stopped flowing. There might have been a problem at the village well or the water treatment plant. So we would do without showers. We would make a meal that didn't require water. We might melt snow if we really got desperate. Sometimes the planes wouldn't come. Things we'd ordered would not arrive. No mail. No big deal. It would come eventually. Sometimes the phones would be down (cell phones were not a viable option in the village when we first moved there). So we wouldn't make any calls. If we wanted to talk to anyone, we'd walk there and speak to them. When you accept the fact that you can't control anything but your own actions and reactions, you don't stress out about these little disruptions. They are always temporary.

We learned to listen to local experience. It never failed us. We learned to embrace new skills. When there are no barber shops for hundreds of miles, you learn to cut your hair. I cut my wife's hair as well as my own—and I got pretty good at it. When there are no restaurants, you learn to cook *everything*. You bake your own bread because it's cheaper and easier to buy flour in bulk (and you don't run the risk of the bread getting moldy before it even gets to you). You learn to repair your clothing, your tools, your vehicles. You have no other options.

And what do you do when the weather is cold and dark and stormy and nobody goes anywhere? Well, you go see people. You visit your neighbor and play some music together. You go to the gym and watch people play basketball (there are usually just as many people at open gym watching and socializing as there are playing, if not more). You finish that book you were reading. You go on a hike because you *need* to get outside every day, even if it's snowing and blowing.

I credit our time in the village as necessary personal growth. Without it, we probably would not be able to do what we are doing now. As noted earlier, we've seen two families move near us, try to do the off-grid thing, and then end in divorces. These marriages were untested in many ways—not that they hadn't had their share of trials, but not the right *kinds* of trials to prepare a marriage for this kind of living. We learned the importance of getting outside for exercise and fresh air—regardless of the weather (that's what cold weather gear is for!). But mostly we learned patience. We already had at least average patience before living in the village—but nothing out of the ordinary. We exercised it. It got stronger. Now we have super patience. One *needs* super patience to be able to thrive living off-grid in Alaska.

Plotting and Planning

Among the things you should plan on packing: several blank notebooks. You will find yourself dreaming of what you will do once winter is over. If I look through my own notebooks, I see clues as to what might end up in yours. Plans for structures, some of which I will never build. But that's okay. The planning is fun. Diagrams of our orchards and which apple varieties can be found in which position of which orchard. First and last frost dates. Diagrams of garden beds and which plants to rotate to and from which beds. Little bits of poetry or song lyrics. General ideas. Notes. Philosophical musings. Lists of what to buy for which building projects. Scale drawings of different additions to the house. Timelines. To-do lists.

You'll need a lot of blank paper.

Most Alaskan gardeners start planning next year's garden well in advance, sometimes even before the new year (by ordering seeds). Once daylight starts returning, you'll find yourself assembling little pots and trays for starting seeds. You'll start a lot of those seeds in the house itself—somewhere near a window. The first sprouts are exciting: green. Photosynthesis freshening the air in your home. Then you'll move them out to the greenhouse (ours is attached to the south side of the house; yours might not be). Once those are out in the greenhouse, you might start even more seeds inside the house and keep moving things out in waves—once the stuff in the greenhouse can go in the ground, the stuff from inside the house goes into the greenhouse, and so on. Some seeds are hardy enough they can be started in the greenhouse while it still freezes at night. It's a good way to make second winter move more quickly.

You'll also be planning your summer camping trips. Fishing trips. Road trips. You'll find budgets popping up in the columns of those pages. Mini business plans. There is no shortage of time for dreaming.

Busying Your Hands

These are things to do when sitting down. It might be in a comfy chair by the fire. It might be on the front porch during summer. Activities to be done while sitting are relaxing, and they keep your hands busy. You might want to start with whittling. It's a good way to satisfy creative urges while creating good fire starter material. While your knife is out, go ahead and sharpen it. Work your way up to wood carving. Get out a needle and thread and make some mittens out of those hares you hunted. Fix your socks. Make a new hat with flappy flaps. Keep your ears warm. Mend your nets. Crochet or knit. Sing songs while you're doing it.

Draw some pictures. Paint. Reload some bullets. Clean your rifle.

Or you can do things that aren't creative or productive but might be a good idea anyway. Finish that sudoku book. Play some solitaire. Play cards or games with other humans, if you have them (humans, that is). All of these are good brain exercise—and they're fun. That's a win-win situation right there.

Outdoors

Of course, there are the obvious outdoor activities—hunting, fishing, hiking, snowshoeing, and all that. You already know about those. There are some you might not know about.

- Sledding and sliding: Downhill sledding is still a lot of fun. You don't have to be a kid to enjoy it. I just did it yesterday. Also, you don't even need a sled to do it. You can just sit down on the snow and slide. Of course, it helps for the hill to be steeper and well-packed. Snow will definitely go up your jacket. That's half the fun.

- Log rolling: Yes, people do this. Mostly in Southeast Alaska.
- Ice floe jumping: A springtime tradition in some parts of the state. When the sea ice starts to break into chunks, hop from one chunk to the next. Some people try to make it across entire bays like this. It quickly becomes a distance competition.
- Ice racing: When certain bodies of water freeze thick enough, people create racecourses for their automobiles and hold ice races.
- Ice darts: It's like playing darts but with icicles. You can't use a regular dart board—it has to be more like an archery target. There have also been many impromptu icicle fencing competitions.
- Ice fetch: Have you ever played fetch with a dog while standing on glare ice? It's a lot more entertaining than the regular kind. Dogs don't have good traction on glare ice.
- Aurora viewing: Watching the Aurora Borealis.
- Aurora tripping: Watching the Aurora Borealis after having stayed up for several days—just so you can hallucinate. Some people prefer to use psychedelic shortcuts to hallucination. I've known several people who swear that the Aurora was reaching down to grab them and take them off into space. That doesn't sound like a lot of fun.
- Aurora conceiving: There is a particular Asian country in which there is a strong belief that conceiving a child during a strong Aurora will bring good luck. Or maybe some kind of superhero child? Anyway, you'll note that certain resorts cater specifically to wealthy people from that country, having all of their signs in that language as well. I'm not saying which country it is because I don't want people thinking I'm making fun of them. I just don't think there's anything to the superstition. Either way, they are very busy during Aurora events.
- Aurora Taunting: This one is mostly for kids. You just taunt the Aurora by whistling at it. A lot of people think it's a bad thing to do. They try to discourage the kids from doing it but

those rebels just do it anyway. And they wonder why bad luck comes…

- Axe throwing: Also more popular in Southeast Alaska (and places where there are lumberjack demonstrations/competitions).
- Snow shoveling: How else are you going to get around the yard in winter? Make a game of it.
- Snow diving: This is nothing more than finding large snow banks near enough to tall things from which you can jump into that snow bank. It might be off a roof. You might try doing tricks, like a front flip. It's like the diving board at the pool but a little bit more freestyle. And into snow.

Fun with Wildlife

Fun with wildlife often has its roots in boredom, usually because there are either too many or too few people in a specific and remote place. Consider: a lonely old dude by himself in the deep woods will get bored and start looking to local wildlife for entertainment. The opposite can be true: a large group of people in a remote camp will also get bored and look to local wildlife for entertainment—and they egg each other on. Between them, they have come up with enough games for a new kind of Olympics.

The solitary kind:

- I've known people that tame local birds. Some people leave food out specifically to see what will come around regularly to eat it. It could be a squirrel. That's been done. More likely it will be a magpie, jay, or a raven. Corvids (a family of which all three bird species are members) have excellent memories, communicate with each other, and pass on cultural information to younger generations. They make excellent pets, especially because you don't *really* have to feed them. A few scraps here and there will do.
- Speaking of ravens, ravens can speak. Anyone who has been around them will have stories of being outside walking around somewhere when they hear a voice—one they *swear* is a human voice. They'll stop and listen carefully until they hear it again and will usually figure out that it's actually a raven (otherwise they'll think the woods are haunted or

something). Ravens can make a lot of different sounds. Most are the typical "caw" kind, but many sound very human. Walter Wilson, who lived in my neck of the woods starting in the territorial days, was reported to have listened enough to figure out what some of the different sounds meant. He was able to make some of the sounds himself, but only the human-esque ones. He tried carrying on conversations with limited success and described it as "…like trying to talk to a Harvard professor when you have the vocabulary of a 2-year-old. You know what you want to say but your mouth just can't make the sounds."

- Ravens aren't the only Alaskan species with sounds that people can come really close to matching. Moose calling is a hobby for many and a passion for few. Most people use it for hunting purposes only—they call a moose to get it close enough for a good shot. But there are others that just do it for fun. Some do it just to see how good they can get at it. A guy from Sterling named Jack Spencer (who lives very near the Kenai Moose Range, as a matter of fact) will do it for pure entertainment. He's constructed a very comfortable tree stand where he can sit and watch for hours on end. He will spend most of September and part of October up there—calling different moose with different calls. There are a number of different kinds of calls—some to attract a mate, some to warn a competitor, some to repel a potential mate (when it turns out there's a more desirable mate nearby), and more—and these calls are all different depending on the moose's gender. He'll use these to see how many moose he can get in one place. That's how he started, anyway, as a personal challenge: how many moose can I get in my yard? Then he started messing with the moose, trying to get different ones to fight each other, different ones to mate with each other, and various combinations thereof (depending on how many moose were around). He said that it was like ventriloquism in a way—trying to throw your voice so it sounds like it's coming from somewhere else. And it's also like putting on a puppet show—trying to control all of these creatures that can really be entertaining but aren't always easy to work with. More than once he's had to sleep in his moose stand because certain aggressive males wouldn't go away. And some of the neighbors say he tries to use his moose calls to get some of the prettier females to mate with *him*. I wouldn't be surprised. He's not a good-looking man and would have a hard time finding a mate among humans (a very nice guy, though—at least he was when I talked to him). Last I heard he was trying to use food to get a particular one to come around more often and stay in a little shed he'd made—for cuddling purposes only. While it wouldn't be the first time a moose had become domesticated, it would be the first time a moose had been domesticated solely to be a companion animal. Why doesn't he just get a dog? He's just obsessed with moose, I suppose.

- There was recently a trapper of limited intelligence that had been hearing tales of a wolverine that was supposedly able to take down a full-grown bull moose. Now this is a guy that moved to the bush because he thought doing so would be a sure way to get his own reality TV show. He'd been an MMA fighter when he was a little bit younger and liked being in the spotlight. He set up a trail camera in a little clearing and would go sit there for a couple of hours every morning, right at sunrise, hoping the wolverine would show up and he could "take it down" somewhere within the camera's field of view (he thought it would be sure to get him his own show, like a "man vs. wild" kind of thing but where man is *literally* fighting wildlife). Fall turned to winter and nothing happened until one morning he got so cold that he stopped moving—just froze right there waiting for the wolverine to show up. Here's the best part, though: when troopers were watching the footage from the trail camera, they saw a wolverine come through several times, including twice when this guy was sitting and waiting. In fact, the second time, he said, "What are you doing back here again, Mr. Beaver?" That's right: he thought the wolverine was a beaver (at least that's what the troopers told me). He didn't even know what a wolverine *looked* like—and he was trying to become a trapper. So he literally froze to death while sitting and waiting for Hugh Jackman to show up so he could challenge Wolverine to a fight.

The group kind:

- To understand this sport, one must first get a little historical context: there is a type of winter boot, commonly worn in Alaska, that is known as the "bunny boot." They are the most durable and most warm of all winter boots. They're inflatable. Steel-toed. Fireproof. White. (There are black versions that are not as good that are known as "Mickey" boots because they resemble the footwear worn by a certain cartoon mouse.) Bunny boots became popular with North Slope oil workers during the 1970s pipeline boom. One spring day (so the story goes), a couple of guys in one of the camps were complaining about the weight of their boots when another member of their group chided them for being wimps. He said something along the lines, "Who cares if they're heavy? Your feet can take anything. You can walk right up to a porcupine and kick him and nothing with happen to your foot." It just so happened that there *was* a porcupine visible through the window of the cafeteria, so the speaker was challenged to put it to the test. Not one to back down, he trotted out onto the packed snow toward the dumpster that sat beside the next building (the porcupine was trying to get into the dumpster, apparently). Now keep in mind that porcupines are slow creatures, not quick to get out of harm's way. You can see any Alaskan highway littered with their carcasses every fall. And this guy ran straight up to the porcupine and gave it a swift kick. It flew against the side of the dumpster, *clang*, before falling on its back, stunned, and then righting itself and scurrying away. This is how the sport of porcupine punting was born. Of course, it isn't really punting—they don't drop kick the porcupines—but "porcupine punting" sounds a lot better than just "porcupine kicking." It has evolved to include a field with distance markings, kind of like a discus or javelin range, but on snow. They trap live porcupines just for weekend games. They put a bit of food at the tee-off point, or line of scrimmage, or whatever you call the place from which they kick the porcupine. The let the animal out of the

trap, it heads for the food, and a contestant runs up and boots it into the field. They take a measurement and mark it down. The porcupine is usually okay—they just let them wander off, probably to be trapped again at some point. A good weekend might have 5 or 6 porcupine puntings. Each camp keeps track of its stats throughout the season (early March through early May), then the champ from each camp competes in a final during Memorial Day weekend. The current record for a kick is 53 feet. Sometimes a guy will get lucky with a good roll after the porcupine lands. It's also a game of chance: there's no telling how big your porcupine is going to be.
As far as anyone knows, there has yet to be a pair of bunny boots damaged from porcupine punting.

- In a similar spirit of testosterone-fueled one-upmanship, a recent trend has developed based on the popularity of the "selfie" and the fact that hibernating bears can sleep through just about anything. This is far less organized and there are no real rules, but the idea is this: find a bear denning site. Sneak in. Take a selfie of yourself posing with the bear(s). There aren't necessarily points awarded or anything like that, but different poses gain different amounts of respect (or "cred") based on difficulty, much like in other extreme sports. It supposedly started with a photo on a wall in a bar in Kodiak: somebody in the 1970s had taken the original bear selfie using a Polaroid. But because Polaroids aren't well-suited to selfies (they are too zoomed-in compared to a person's arm length, by default), the picture showed part of a man's face and part of a bear. Nobody could say for sure if it was a live bear or not, but the legend behind the photo was that it was indeed taken in a bear den (or so the label next to the photo said). Many debates about the photo have taken place over the years, but in 2011, somebody decided to see if it could really be done—and they would find out by replicating the photo (but with better quality). After the first photo was a viral hit (at least in Alaska), more people started trying, and not just in Kodiak. People would do it in costume. One guy very carefully put a pointy party hat on the bear (he just set it on there, he didn't stretch the strap around the bear's chin or anything). Another guy that calls himself "Cuddlin' Cody" poses in different positions where he is either spooning a bear or being spooned. Legend has it that one time he was so comfortable that he actually fell asleep that way for an entire night. Now that people are sharing videos on social media as much as they do photos, we're seeing just that: people competing by seeing who can take the longest video (Cuddlin' Cody is still the reigning champ there, even though none of his current videos are as long as his legendary snooze is supposed to have been). It sounds crazy and dangerous, but I'll admit that morbid curiosity makes me wonder how cozy it would actually be. While technically an individual activity, the social nature of sharing the photos and videos makes it more of a group thing. Yes, even grown ups can double-dog-dare each other into doing some incredibly stupid things.

Summer Activities

This could just as easily be titled "Fun with tourists." The obvious summer activities would be thinks like fishing, festivals, camping, and gardening. The less obvious:

- Giving bad directions: Even though there aren't that many roads in Alaska, people seem to get lost easily. A lot of our roads aren't labeled and/or don't register on a car's navigation system. So when a tourist asks you for directions, think about the most bizarre place you can send them. There are plenty of out-of-the-ordinary places in Alaska that are only here because you wouldn't find them anywhere else (because people can pretty much do whatever they want to do in Alaska). These can include new age retreat centers, militia headquarters, religious cults, pot farms, musk ox farms, yak farms, and beet farms. Memorize where these are so you can send people there. Or send them to a local oil rig or to the craziest old coot you can think of. They're here to experience the real Alaska, right? Then show them.
- Telling tall tales: Some people will believe anything you tell them about Alaska. It's a big and impressive place. People here must lead big and impressive lives, right? Tell them about that time a bear tried to steal your fish and you

responded by stealing its cub (side note: my grandfather actually did bring a black bear cub home once—but it was an orphan. He didn't steal it. And my grandmother would not let him keep it.). Tell them about the time you were fishing on your buddy's boat and were pulling in a king salmon but a beluga whale was attached to it and didn't want to give it up, so you did your best whale speech and actually convinced the beluga to let go of the salmon already. Then it was all torn up with bite marks so you tossed it back and the beluga took it down, laughing at you. So you told it, in whale talk, to buzz off and he came back with some buddies and it was on. You can use all kinds of material—shipwrecks (lots of those), Spanish explorers (who must have also been pirates, of course), crash sites of old Soviet spy crafts or WWII Japanese fighter jets, little people of the tundra, anything to do with wildlife, entire ghost villages (because of epidemics of one kind of another), crazy gold miners acting like crazy gold miners (there have been massacres due to that), stories of people that got cabin fever and ended up adopting a small pack of coyotes so as to not be so lonely, people that moved to the backwoods to escape Y2K and are still there, waiting. We have it all. Enough bizarre stuff happens in Alaska on a regular basis that it isn't too hard to elaborate to hilarity.

- Bug swatting: It's strange to think that people would find ways of turning mosquitoes into entertainment, but it happens. Some people like to sit out on the porch and swat with those electrified bug zappers (they look like tennis rackets). It's a lot more fun than bug zappers where you don't actually hit the bugs. Others will have contests. One such contest goes as follows: a small group of people goes outside and waits for a predetermined amount of time (perhaps 1-5 minutes). They form a bit of a circle, almost like a conga line, and at the end of the time limit each person will slap the back of the person in front of them. Then they count the number of dead mosquitoes to see who wins (whoever has the most mosquitoes is the sweetest, and therefore champion). This also works for midges (a.k.a. no-see-ums).

- Drinking games: Spend some time at any bar or restaurant during summer (tourist season). Anytime you get asked a particularly stereotypical question (or hear particular comments), that's a drink. Some common questions/comments:
    - Do you know where Sarah Palin lives?
    - How can you be wearing a t-shirt right now? It's only 50 degrees out!
    - Would you like to see the picture of the moose we saw yesterday?
    - We saw a moose yesterday!
    - Can you see Russia from here?
    - I thought everyone was going to be living in igloos!
    - Why aren't you wearing a gun? Aren't you scared of bears?!?
    - What do you do when it's dark for 24 hours?

The bottom line is that necessity, the mother of invention, has so far created all kinds of ways for people to preserve their sanity in extreme situations.

Chapter Ten: Safety

Things can get pretty hairy in the bush. Bear hairy. Or moose hairy. Or maybe just "unwelcome visitor" hairy. That's why most of us usually carry around a very large gun. Not only does it need to be so large that you can barely lift it, it also needs to shoot several rounds per second. That's right. You need a Gatling gun. No bear has ever been taken out by anything else.

Or you could just use some common sense and not have to tote around a giant sidearm all the time. I only carry a firearm on very rare occasions. Why not carry all the time? I don't need it. It's pretty easy to know when I will need it, so I save myself the trouble and leave it in its place unless I know I'll need it (some like to also keep one in their vehicle—just don't forget to declare it if you ever get pulled over). The only people I see walking around with a big pistol are people that either live in the city (and are visiting our neck of the woods) or have just moved to the area. I've hiked all over the state for a decade now and never needed a gun for my safety. I'll carry a rifle if I happen to be hunting, but that's never been *needed* for protection.

There has been a lot written about how to use guns—whether for hunting or protection or both. This chapter will be mostly about how to avoid being in a situation where you need one at all (and how to know when a situation arises that will actually require one). Like I said, the majority of us that live here prefer to go about our day unencumbered. While most people carrying a big pistol are usually outsiders or newcomers, I have noticed something else: most cars that feature NRA stickers and pro-gun bumper stickers have out-of-state license plates. It isn't that Alaskans don't like our guns. We do. It's that guns are not a big deal. They're a part of life. Everyone has them and everyone uses them. Nobody is telling anyone *not* to use them. Nobody feels like their gun ownership is threatened. The whole thing is a giant non-issue. So while most of us don't feel the need to advertise on our cars, we also don't feel the need to make a statement by carrying (as I've seen some people do in the lower states). We just assume everyone has a gun in the car. We know there's almost always a gun in any home. If anything, we get suspicious if someone *doesn't* own one: it usually means they aren't allowed to own one because of a violent criminal record.

Anecdote: Duck, Duck, Bear

In all of my years of living in Alaska, I've fired a total of one bullet for the sake of protection. One. It was in the middle of the night on Mother's Day weekend (at that time of year, there isn't much darkness at night, but this occurred during that short dark stretch), and a recently-woken and hungry spring bear found its way into our yard and began to test the fence that surrounded our chicken and duck yard. The dogs knew he was there. They started going nuts. I didn't know what was outside, so I told them to stay put and I went out to see. With my headlamp on, I was able to make out a figure pushing on the fence. At first it kind of looked like a person. It's movements were strange. He was upright. It seemed like an ape—maybe a gorilla. But I know there are no gorillas in Alaska.

At this point, he'd already taken one duck and was coming back for a second (I didn't learn that until later). I went back inside and got a gun ready to go. I let the dogs out. It isn't that I don't love my dogs—I do. I wasn't sending them into danger. They're smart enough to not get too close. I've seen them do it enough times with moose—they'll stay at a safe distance and bark. They use their physical presence as a mental reminder to the wild things that they should not move any closer. My dogs would be a buffer between the bear and me—a noisy buffer with bared teeth. The three of them ran over, semi-surrounding the bear, bluff charging, then retreating. The bear did the same.

The dogs were keeping the bear roughly in one place. I came out with a gun in my hand, headlamp on, taking careful steps and not wanting to get too far from the house. I needed to be near enough to the door that I could run into the house faster than the bear could get from his location to mine. I steadied my arm, taking aim with the open sights, aiming at the flash of my headlamp in the bears eyes. But it was hard. A dog would jump in front. The bear would shift. I couldn't just aim at the bear. I also needed to watch my dogs, think about their positions, look at the directions in which they were moving. I adjusted the shot so it would probably hit the bear but definitely wouldn't hit one of my dogs. I squeezed the trigger and it went boom. The bear turned tail and ran the other direction.

I don't know if I hit him or not. I probably didn't. I'm sure I erred on the side of caution and shot farther from my dogs than necessary. Either way, the bear didn't come back. Mission accomplished. With that in mind, a .22 would have done just as well—turns out that a loud *bang* was all that was needed. Furthermore, I didn't need to have a gun ready to go in some secret compartment by my bed—I had plenty of time to assess the situation and even put an earplug in my right ear before shooting. That isn't to say that there aren't times when a gun comes in handy at a moment's notice—but you're likely live an entire lifetime without ever actually being in such a situation, so don't go stressing yourself out about being prepared to shoot without having time to think about the situation and come up with a plan.

Bears

Bears are awesome creatures. They're big. They look nice. Cuddly? To some, apparently. I sometimes wish I had a domesticated bear to play with. Most of all, they're predictable. It's easy to know where they are going to be at what times of the year (eating fresh greens in the forest in spring, eating fish from the river in summer, eating berries on the muskeg in fall). It's easy to know what times of day they are most active (early morning and late evening). It's easy to know what spooks them and keeps them from coming around. This is not rocket science.

Like many wild creatures, they have excellent hearing and sense of smell. Like many wild creatures, they want nothing to do with humans. So we combine those two ideas to come up with a strategy to keep them away: you need to sound and smell like a human wherever you go. That's pretty easy, actually. You talk loudly. You sing songs if needed. Having dogs with you is an extra bonus. Bears don't like them, either. And dogs are even louder than people. They also stink.

I may brag about never having encountered bears while out in nature. That doesn't mean that bears weren't there. I've come across bear tracks (fresh ones) on a number of occasions. I've come across bear poop (also fresh) on a number of occasions. These things don't send me running for home. They are signs that my noise, smell, and dogs are doing their job. A bear was near. It knew we were coming. It left.

There is also safety in numbers. If your sound and smell isn't enough to deter some bear from randomly approaching and eating you, then having more people in your group will help. Bears are much less likely to stick around when the group is larger. Somebody once told me that there has never been a bear attack (in Alaska) when it was a group of 4 or more people. I don't know if that's true. It might not be—the guy that told it to me was kind of an idiot. Regardless, it's a good idea to stay together as a group.

I did have a close encounter with a bear—once. As a 6-year-old child. It wasn't even in Alaska. But a black bear was interested in a fish my oldest brother had just pulled out of a river. He didn't catch the fish—it was already dead, floating downstream, and he literally pulled it out of the river. I grew tired of watching him fish, so I turned from the river to walk into the woods and froze in my steps—there was a bear right in front of me, no more than 6 feet away. I tried to get my brother's attention, but he didn't believe me at first. I said, "Umm…there's a bear right here." He wouldn't turn around—he just waved his hand above his head, saying, "Oh, hi Mr. Bear." So I was the only thing standing between this bear and a very pungent fish. By the time I convinced my oldest brother to turn around, our *other* brother returned from his own wanderings in the woods, sized up the situation, and started throwing rocks at the bear. It looked kind of fun, and we, in general, are people that enjoy throwing things at targets. So we all started throwing rocks at the bear. And sticks. And pine cones. And whatever else was handy. And the bear started moving away, and we kept doing it. We then thought it would be a good idea to chase after the bear. We ended up chasing it through the woods for about a quarter of a mile until it came across a group of tourists, got spooked, and climbed a tree. The tourists loved it. We loved it. The bear didn't love it. Rangers eventually captured it and moved it to an area with fewer people.

Very few bear encounters will result in actual physical contact. Whether you prefer a gun or bear spray as a last resort, make sure you know how to use it when the time comes. If I'm going to be out by myself in bear territory in the early morning or at dusk, and it isn't winter, I will probably bring something for protection. The only time I might find myself in such a situation is if I'm hunting. In that case, I'll already be armed. But I won't be practicing good bear etiquette, either—I'll be quiet. I will try not to have any noticeable smell. I won't have my dogs with me. I might even be alone (though I prefer hunting with a friend).

There are other ways of deterring interested bears before it comes down to shooting one. The well-known methods are making noise, making yourself look big, and throwing things. These can and do work. Some people like to have one of those air horns handy—they're really loud and can spook a bear at a moment's notice. If you do happen to hunt alone and on foot, it might be a smart thing to bring along.

Moose

You are far more likely to be harmed by a moose than by a bear—statistically, that is. Moose are far more abundant, can be just as big or bigger, and can even be aggressive. They're also less likely to be timid around people.

Just like with bears, you'll find that mother moose are protective of their young. If you get between a mother and a baby, expect to be charged. If you get near the young in general (even if it isn't between), expect to be charged. If you're too close to bulls when they're fighting with each other or rutting, expect to be charged. They don't mess around—they're busy and you're interfering.

In most situations, you can just move away and that will be sufficient—they will stop moving toward you. But the might not. So if you're near a moose and it makes a move like it wants to hurt you, your move should not just be *away* from the moose, but also in the direction of some kind of shelter. If you just run into an open area, that moose will be on you in short order. They can really run fast.

Humans have few advantages over moose in these situations. The only real advantages we have are quick thinking and dexterity. We can climb while they can't. We can open doors while they can't. We can stop and change directions more quickly. So be aware of your surroundings. Is there a vehicle or structure you can enter quickly? Something you can climb? Move toward those things. Trees are handy for more than just climbing. Legend has it that if you move to the opposite side of a tree, you can keep circling around the tree, always keeping it between yourself and the moose. Don't worry about looking like an idiot running in circles around a tree. The moose is probably the only one that can see you, and they aren't known for being judgmental. I have not tried this method personally. I *have* had to quickly run into one of my sheds or into a vehicle, but I was never really in that much danger. Regardless, when you see a moose turn and move toward you, it will be scary. Remember: they do not hunt. They only defend themselves. Just don't make them mad and everything will be fine (whereas you might come across a predatory bear, though they are rare).

Moose are more dangerous on roadways. They will try darting (or ambling) across roads whenever they feel like it. They might run in front of your vehicle. They might run into the side. Cars don't seem to make much sense to them. If cars were obviously dangerous to moose, there would be far fewer moose collisions. So be extra cautious driving in moose territory, especially in the evening and at night. They tend to be thicker near rivers. Many highways feature signs in areas known to have a lot of moose (it just looks like a road sign with a moose on it). If it's a snowy winter and there are large berms of snow beside the road, you may find that moose would rather walk on the road than through deep snow. It's obviously easier walking. So be extra careful in those conditions as well.

Many drivers (and passengers) will not survive a collision with a moose. It depends on the speed of the collision and how the moose falls. If it falls on the roof or the hood of the vehicle, it can be very dangerous. The moose are obviously large enough to crush a person. And if a moose lands on your hood with its legs pointing toward the car, you need to duck and duck fast—it will kick its legs. Moose kicks to sensitive areas (like human heads and torsos) are often deadly.

Otherwise, moose are great. Unless they're eating your garden. But they're cute. Fun to watch. Tasty. They can be tamed, but it's not worth it (and not legal in Alaska, actually). Just let them be wildlife and things will be fine.

Humans

Statistically, humans are potentially more dangerous to you than moose are. What?!? That's crazy! Human are dangerous to each other? They might hurt each other? Well, sometimes it's accidental. Sometimes it's not. Whenever I meet someone that asks me how I can live in Alaska when there are bears around, I wonder how they can live in the city with all those people around. That's a lot more dangerous. I'll take bears over people any day. People are less predictable. They don't hibernate. They might make elaborate plans to hurt you. They'll also say nasty things on social media that might hurt your feelings. Yep. I'll take bears any day.

Probably the most common danger is humans behind the wheel of automobiles. Especially during the cold time of year. We can get some very slippery roads at times, and not everyone drives a safe speed in those conditions. So crashes happen. The best way to avoid these problems is to not drive when the roads are bad. But sometimes driving can't be avoided. In that case, be prepared by having a vehicle to match the conditions. Four-wheel-drive is a must. Most people also keep a set of studded tires for winter use (see the chapter on transportation). Learning how to get out of a skid or a slide is a must. Don't worry—you'll get practice. Try to do it at slow speeds on empty roads until you get the hang of it. You also need to learn how to "read" the road and drive on the right part. Sometimes that might be the part that is most packed down by other vehicles. Sometimes it might be the opposite—that will depend on conditions and if the denser snow has become hard-packed and slippery.

Other accidental dangers might be in firearm use and fire safety in general. A lot of people move to Alaska and are a bit too excited about shooting some guns. They might not think about what else (other than a target) might be in the direction that they are shooting. And a lot of people want to have bonfires and barbeques when conditions aren't safe. Alaska typically has more wildfire acreage than any other state in any given year. People don't think of it being a dry place, but it can dry out pretty quickly—especially in May and June. So pay attention to (and respect) burn bans, and always make sure there is defensible space around your home (space clear of flammable vegetation). Wildfires are particularly scary because we don't have the kinds of emergency services found in lower states—you might live very far from a fire station, and there aren't going to be any fire hydrants by your home. You are at the mercy of nature and of your neighbors, so hope that your neighbors make smart choices. If they don't, you can help educate them.

Alaska attracts a lot of different people for a lot of different reasons. A surprising number of people move to "the end of the road" (or even past the end) to get away from a checkered past. Some bring their bad habits with them—these can be anything. It's easy enough to find out. And it's a lot easier to get to know your neighbors when you don't have to worry about whether or not they're hiding a very big secret, so don't hesitate to do a background check if something doesn't add up. For looking up neighbors that have lived in Alaska for along time, there's a state-run website known as "court view" that gives public access to all existing court records in Alaska—even things as minor as a speeding ticket. Some people that use this site to snoop on others tend to assume the worst, so it's good to keep something in mind: being charged with something is not the same as being guilty of something. We have our trial system the way it is for a reason, and it's a big step up from the days when an accusation was enough to ruin (or end) someone's life—especially if that accusation came from someone with higher social standing. Online research is a great help if someone has a clearly awful record. Even so, they may end up being a neighbor that will help you out in time of need. You *can* be neighborly without having to be close friends. Ideally you can be both—just use good judgment and know that a lot of people think of Alaska as a fresh start. Some will find it is just that (and good for them!), but those that can't keep on the up-and-up will quickly find themselves unwelcome.

Dogs

I'm a dog person. I don't mean that I'm half-dog, half-human. That would be weird. And impossible. Maybe it would be better to call myself a "person that likes dogs." Is that less confusing? Perhaps. But I do like dogs. They're great pets. They're cuddly and can help you keep warm. They're good for your mental and emotional health. They can be good entertainment (remember "ice fetch"?). They can be trained to work—whether it be hunting or herding or hauling. And they're also great for security.

Most people that live off-grid do not have home security systems. Those usually require constant power, and anything that requires constant power tends to go by the wayside when you don't have the ability to plug in to the predictable grid. Some people use trail cameras (game cameras) for keeping an eye on who is coming and going from the area, but those aren't really helpful when something is going down *right now* (good to have, though, especially if you leave for long periods of time). That's where dogs come in. They are living alarms. If someone unfamiliar approaches, they bark. This alerts you to the person's presence, and it also alerts that person that there are dogs around. Dogs aren't always friendly to unfamiliar people. Dogs have been used in this way for millennia, and for good reason. It works.

Some professional criminals have ways of dealing with dogs, but you're unlikely to ever have anyone like that coming around (and bringing a steak to bribe your dogs with, or whatever method they use). But if you want to get really paranoid about it, I know of some people that have employed a "zone dog" system. They have a dog (or dogs) in different zones, separated from each other by doors and walls. They might have an outside dog or two that only come inside as far as the entry way (through a dog door). Then they might have a dog or two inside the house. If some criminal mastermind happens to plan for dogs, they might not be planning for separate sets of dogs at every step of the way. Most criminals are not very smart and many are opportunistic. They're not going to mess with your stuff if it's a lot more difficult than anyone else's.

Dogs are also great when it comes to protecting you from potentially dangerous wildlife. They can keep bears and moose away. Not many dogs are going to be aggressive toward those animals (though bear dogs do exist), but they'll at least stand their ground and maybe annoy the animal long enough for it to lose interest and leave. When I had the bear come and take a duck, my dogs didn't chase it off, but they held it in place long enough for me to take action. The bear didn't seem too threatened by them, but it also didn't have any interest in committing to an attack.

In my experience, there are only three downsides to dogs: they require food, they like to roll in poop, and they tend to get too close to porcupines. Pulling quills out of a dog can be a very trying task. But you just have to hold the dog down, grab some pliers, and be quick but accurate (having another person to help hold the dog makes a big difference). The quills do come out (and you don't need to cut the ends off with scissors—that's just an old wive's tale). Some might not need to come out right away (depending on location), so you might need to do it in multiple sessions. I've had to remove dozens from a single encounter—including quills lodged in my dog's gums. But you'll get through it. It's a good idea to get some toothache medicine (you know, the stuff you're supposed to put on your teeth if you have a toothache?) to deaden the area for your dog. That will make it a lot easier to pull them out of the mouth area.

As for rolling in poop, there's not a lot to be done for that. You just have to wash the dog. Or shave it.

Weather

At certain times of year, the weather can be dangerous. You could be struck by lightning. A big wind might blow a tree down on top of you. Hailstones might pepper you with bruises. Floodwaters can sweep your home away. These are all quite rare, though. The more obvious dangers are the winter ones: cold, snow, and ice.

Ice is becoming a more and more common danger, especially in the more populated part of Alaska. Warmer winters bring more rain—but the nighttime temperature usually drops low enough for that rain to turn into ice. In fact, our schools don't have snow days. They have ice days (okay, there are occasional snow days, but they are very rare). On ice days, it is expected that dozens of cars will end up in the ditches alongside all the major roads in Southcentral Alaska. People don't drive unless they absolutely have to. Again, studded tires are a must. Sometimes our road has ice several inches thick. Tire chains might even be better at times.

It's good to put chains (or studs) on your feet as well. I usually slip and fall hard about once every winter or so. I know a lot of people that have had serious injuries—broken bones and concussions—due to ice slippage. It's extremely common. One of my neighbors recently slipped on the ice near his house and knocked himself out. He lives alone. He regained consciousness but had no idea how long he had been out. It obviously wasn't very long—if it had been long at all, he would have frozen to death. Ice cleats can keep these things from happening (though sometimes I will slip even in ice cleats, depending on the type). Some people make homemade cleats by using small screws. Some buy fancy cleats. I prefer those with straps—they're easy to lose when you're walking around, and the ones with straps tend to stay on better. Don't skimp on these. Get good ones that will dig into the ice and grip well.

Snow isn't usually much of a hazard. We expect it and are prepared for it. But there are some times when it is so abundant that it causes some serious problems. When combined with wind, drifts can grow ten feet tall overnight. I've seen it happen. Sometimes it's just so snowy that people can't get anywhere. Plow trucks aren't effective because they either can't get through the snow or they have nowhere to push it. In the winter of 2011-2012 (a very snowy winter in this part of the state), a lot of people had to hire front-end loaders to clear roads. That's a bit more pricey than a plow truck. But not having road access can be serious—emergency vehicles can't get to emergencies. Hope you don't have one when the snow falls hard. Having a snowmachine might be better during such times.

Heavy and drifting snow can cause other unexpected problems. Some people's greenhouse roofs cave in. The wind might blow snow into your vehicle's tailpipe, clogging it up. Drifts might cover the places where your home is supposed to vent fumes to the outside (like from water heaters, propane furnaces, or oil-burning heaters). Depending on conditions, drifts can also get really hard and cement-like. You might try to drive through one and find that it's like driving into a wall. It's a good idea to always have several days' worth of supplies at all times, just in case it takes that long to dig out after a storm.

Cold can creep up on you. Sometimes you don't even know you're supposed to be prepared for it. Take driving, for example: you might not wear much winter clothing in your car because you'll have the heater on, and the place you're headed will also be heated. You only need clothes enough to get you from the door to the car to the door. But when there are car troubles or a car accident, it gets serious. If you roll your car into a ditch miles from anywhere, you're in for a long, cold walk. Sometimes people don't survive these. Waiting for other drivers to pass might not work. You phone might not work. It's easier just to be ready for cold. Have an emergency kit in your car. These vary, but usually include cold weather gear, flares, food, emergency blankets, jack, lug wrench, and so on.

When people are being active in the outdoors during winter, they tend to dress for the occasion. In these situations, there are only a few things to remember:

- Don't let yourself get sweaty.
- Don't stop and rest for too long.

- Make sure people know where you are planning to be at what times (in case your snowmachine breaks down, a snowshoe breaks, the weather changes, you get injured, etc.).
- Don't trust ice when crossing rivers and creeks. Test it.
- Beware of overflow: if river water is flowing on top of the ice, don't cross if you're on foot. Find a better way. Don't get frozen feet. (Some people cross anyway, then immediately build a fire to thaw/dry feet and socks and boots, but only when crossing overflow is unavoidable.)
- Learn to "swim" out of deep snow. I have found myself in snow so deep and soft that I could not extract myself the usual way. You have to literally swim out of it. You get your body as horizontal as possible and start crawling, almost like it's quicksand. Digging yourself out might be another option, but that depends on the character of the snow.

In short, just make sure you can handle any hazards so you aren't out too long. No matter how good your gear is, you won't want to be out all night in it. Not unless you want to build a snow shelter and a fire. That's some hardcore survival stuff right there.

Cold can be dangerous at home, too. In some cases, living on-grid is actually more dangerous. When there are extended power outages, some people are unable to heat their homes (they may have nothing more than an oil-burning heater or some other heat source that requires electricity). Not every home is wired to be backed up with a generator, so some people are at the mercy of the utility companies. They can't heat their home until the power comes back on. These power outages are common, especially in winter (and especially when ice is accumulating on everything). Sometimes people that heat with wood will just run out of firewood.

What do you do when the temperature drops and the wind howls and you can't keep the temperature up? Even if you have a lot of firewood, there are some times that you can be running your woodstove full blast and the house still loses heat. If the wind and cold show no signs of letting up, you need to do something else. Something more. Maybe you're okay with baking some cookies at 2 in the morning. The extra boost of heat from your oven might be what you need. Eating is also a good idea—food keeps you warm. You will need the fuel (and if you can keep that heat trapped close to your body, all the better). Some people will build themselves a nest—a burrow that is so thick that body heat will keep it heated through the night no matter what the conditions (not a bad backup plan, but not ideal). Sometimes people will run a generator to power a space heater (of course, generators might be finicky when the temperatures are very low). Just be wary of any propane space heater—I've known people to use these indoors, and it's really not a good idea. They need to be vented properly. Just like with moose attacks, not a year goes by that I don't read a news article about some people that died of carbon monoxide poisoning because something in their home wasn't venting properly (or they tried to run a generator inside). Make sure you have a good CO detector (or two) and that you monitor the batteries.

Communication

So power outages are common. We've covered that. And when that happens, that means your internet is probably not working. You may or may not have cell reception (you may not be in a place that has cell reception even when there *aren't* power outages, though then you'll probably be somewhere that doesn't even have grid power to begin with). Sometimes your safety depends on your ability to communicate to neighbors and/or emergency services.

Remember that network of trails you've been maintaining? Those are great for getting to where you can find other people. Use them if you need to. But what if you're in one of those rare situations when you need help but are not in a position to move yourself? Can you just press a button and alert someone to the fact that you have fallen down and cannot get back up again? Those services don't work in rural Alaska. No, you need a backup. And that backup is radio.

Using radio to communicate assumes that there are other people out there that also use radio to communicate. In much of the United States, that's limited to the occasional amateur radio aficionado, truckers, and emergency responders. We have all of those in Alaska, and more. In coastal areas (with fishing fleets and such), there are radios on the boats. In many villages, VHF radio is the preferred method of communication, with everyone tuned in to the same channel (it's a good source of entertainment as well: just sit back and listen to the radio chatter). We also have a higher per-capita rate of pilots than most places (and more radios on those planes as well). The bottom line is that if you need to send a distress signal or communicate in case of an emergency, using a radio is not a bad way to go. Just make sure that you know what channels/frequencies are commonly used in your area (and for what purposes).

Chapter Eleven: Money

There are two main ways that people living off-grid make their money: starring in reality TV shows and writing books about living off-grid in Alaska. Personally, I've thought about applying to be on different shows—I've been privy to emails from interested production companies. But I don't want my family having to deal with that kind of thing, so I'm writing this book instead. Apart from those ways of making your money, there are a few others worth mentioning.

The issue of money requires thought and planning, and I'd even go so far as to suggest finding a good job before you make any commitments in terms of buying land—even if it's just a seasonal job. Unless you have a bunch of money coming in from a pension or something, you'll need income for a lot of things—food and fuel being at the top of the list. You'll be spending hundreds a month at the very least (not to mention land payments, if you have them), so don't go thinking that you can just move to your wilderness plot and live off the land. It would take an expert in *everything* to be able to do that. In real-life situations, the true experts at surviving in Alaska (Alaska Native peoples) wouldn't live like that. To survive without the engine of civilization bringing you tools and gas requires a village full of people working together. If you are reading this book, you probably aren't an expert in everything. That's okay. You don't need to be one. You just need to get a job. Money will buy you the goods and services that will allow you to get by without needing an entire village full of people with different skill sets.

Trapping

There are still trappers out there. Not many places have the ratio of wildlife to humans that makes trapping profitable, but if you're lucky enough to live in one of those places, it's worth thinking about. In general, though, trapping as a means of income is a thing of the past. People just don't wear fur like they used to. Now that I think of it, most of the clothing I have that contains fur is not the result of trapping (hunting, actually). The exception is a small strip of beaver around the ruff of my parka.

The main upside of trapping is that it's done in winter. That leaves summers open for doing whatever you enjoy.

Commercial Fishing

This is actually a very common way for people to make their living. It's easy to find work and it usually pays well. It definitely favors the young due to its physical nature, but anyone with pertinent experience should do just fine. Just keep your eyes open for announcements from captains looking for crew (these can be online or on local bulletin boards). Once you get your first job, the subsequent jobs are a lot easier to get—assuming you work hard and maintain a good reputation. It's easy to make connections for other (future) work.

Different parts of the state have different seasons for different kinds of fish. Different kinds of fish require different kinds of fishing, but the skills tend to overlap pretty heavily. You could do herring in one part of the state and red salmon in another. There's cod and crab. Pink and chum. Pollock and kings. Most of the work happens during the warm part of the year—that's the main downside. But you don't have to fill your entire summer with different fishing jobs—you could just do one or two.

Mining

Obviously I'm talking about gold. Not many people can run their own copper or diamond mine. But gold mining claims do exist in Alaska. Unlike the old days, it's not possible to make a living just with a gold pan (and even in the old days it was very rare for that ever happen). The entire state has been surveyed (geologically), and any promising leads for gold deposits have been explored. But if you have the right stream coming out of the right mountains, it might be worth your while to do a bit of panning or sluicing.

Otherwise you'll be looking at a miniature version of industrial mining: using heavy equipment to remove "overburden" (what a strange way to think about topsoil…), eventually getting at the ore-bearing layers, grinding it up, separating it, and so on…well, that's a hefty operation. And then you need to find ways of dealing with your mine tailings. You'll probably need loads of permits and have to follow a whole lot of regulations that you might not understand—in short, it would be a full-time lifestyle, in which case you probably should just read a book about small mining operations. Some people do it, and some people do well at it, but the good claims are hard to come by.

It's probably best to just keep the gold pan handy and do it recreationally.

Farming

People do make a living from farming in Alaska—but they are very few. Farming on a commercial scale would require hundreds (or even thousands) of acres in order to make a living. Consider potatoes: Alaskan potatoes sell pretty well—but only in Alaska (the cost of transport outside would make it impossible to compete with much cheaper potatoes from Idaho and Washington). Here they usually cost 50-60 cents per pound at the grocery store. But the farmer doesn't make 50 cents per pound. Even if the farmer *did* make 50 cents per pound, think about how many potatoes you'd have to sell to even average $1,000 of income for each month. That would be 24,000 pounds of potatoes. Are you going to be doing that with a 4-wheeler and a hoe? No. You'd need machinery. You'd need irrigation. You'd need all kinds of really expensive stuff.

Barley would be even more difficult. There is a flour mill in Alaska that mills mostly barley and makes lovely flour. Even though it is grown and processed here in Alaska, it still costs about $2 per pound for regular flour. While it's better flour than most of what you'll find in the grocery store (and healthier, and better for the environment because you're buying local), not many people will buy it when regular wheat flour is only 40 cents per pound. You have to literally pay five times as much to get a product that should, logically, be cheaper. But farmers in Alaska have it hard: our growing season is short. Barley is usually grown in winter in warmer climates (while more profitable crops are grown in summer). Here it is a summer crop—the *only* crop of the year for any given field where it grows.

So staple crops aren't the best for someone looking to make some money from a smaller chunk of land. That doesn't mean you can't make money by growing things. And no, I'm not talking about growing marijuana (which some people do—apparently it's really hard to turn a profit as the grower because they pay most of the taxes). There are other high-value things a person can grow.

Pay attention to the price-per-pound of the things you usually buy at the store. As noted before, things like flour and potatoes don't go for much. But what about honey? That costs *a lot* per pound, and you can definitely keep bees in Alaska. Fresh fruits and vegetables also cost a lot per pound (at least in most parts of the state), often over $3 per pound for the non-organic stuff (and a lot more in bush villages). So if you do grow your own fruits and vegetables, you can easily get $5 per pound if you can market it as organic. People who invest in high tunnels can grow so much produce during the warm season that they might be able to make $25,000 from it in a year (gross). Once you account for time, labor, and materials, that's not something you can retire on, but it is enough to keep you supplied with the necessities (plus a lot of really good food for yourself).

The hard part is finding a market. If you live far from anyone, you won't find many (or any) buyers. But if there's a town within a reasonable distance, it probably has a farmer's market during the warm season. There are even a few farms in semi-rural areas that have CSA (community-supported agriculture) programs, in which people sign up for regular produce deliveries. Some grocery stores will even stock local produce. It takes some legwork and you have to be more than just a farmer—you have to be your own promoter.

If you have expertise on certain value-added products, that can also be a good option. Some people make jams and jellies. Some use local materials to make soaps and beauty products. If you keep bees, you might make things with beeswax. There are a couple of small companies that make products from birch sap (such as syrup). All of these take time, effort, and expertise, but can be rewarding if you enjoy the work. People will also use their farmer's market stalls to sell handicrafts—so if you do fine woodworking or skin sewing, you can have a space for those things as well.

Dairy products can be tricky. While some people may pay plenty for local, organic, raw milk (or local cheeses, etc.), there could be extra legal hurdles. I know there were some people on the Kenai Peninsula that got sick from raw milk in recent years. While I don't think there were any lawsuits, that milk producer was certainly in danger of being sued. That being said, remember that there's a goat farmer in my area that sells goat milk for $15 per gallon. That's a lot. And people buy it. If you like the idea of keeping dairy animals, just make sure you research legal hurdles before you go selling your products.

Firefighting

A lot of people supplement their income by being seasonal firefighters. Alaska needs a lot of seasonal firefighters, actually, as we get plenty of large wildfires every summer. They're far more common in the interior part of the state, but you don't necessarily have to live in the Interior to get these jobs. You can get these jobs through federal agencies (i.e. Bureau of Land Management), the state of Alaska, or even at the local borough level. There's enough fire to go around, and if they don't use you here, you might get shipped out to fight fires in other states when they need the extra personnel. Most of the action in Alaska is centered around McGrath, Fairbanks, Delta Junction, and Tok, but there are different groups stationed in quite a few other places.

The pay is actually pretty good, especially when there are big fires and people have to work lots of overtime. It's difficult work, and obviously very dangerous, but also rewarding (and it will keep you fit). I once thought I'd apply for a summer seasonal firefighting job, so I looked into it. Any applicant needs to be able to pass the "pack test." The pack test requires that you travel (by foot) 5 miles in less than an hour—all while carrying 50 pounds. I gave myself a practice run and found that yes, I could do it. But it wasn't easy. I ended up sticking with the teaching—being a firefighter doesn't seem like a smart choice for a recovering asthmatic.

Like fishing and farming, this job takes up most or all of a summer. That's fine if you want time off in winter for things like skiing or mushing. But if you want freedom in the summer, explore other options first.

"The Slope"

There are any number of jobs a person can get on the North Slope (called "the slope" for short). All of these jobs revolve around the oil fields in some way. Most of the jobs require skilled labor and pay very well. You could be working directly with the wells (i.e. welding), but there are jobs in transportation (driving trucks), management, and all kinds of related services. Some people get jobs as cooks or cleaners in the different camps—even the unskilled labor still pays well.

It is kind of its own little world in that way: all employees live in a camp, cut off from the rest of the world. But nobody lives there year-round. People usually work for two weeks, then take two weeks off (or have some kind of similar schedule with large blocks of work alternating with large blocks of off-time). That means you can work on the slope and live anywhere else in the state, so long as you can get to an airport easily. Some people even live out of state while keeping slope jobs—the travel time isn't a whole lot different, and the cost of living can make a big difference.

Schedule-wise, it's nice to be able to have time off in all seasons. But the work rotation schedule is difficult for many, especially those with families. The environment is also some of the harshest to be found in all of Alaska: constant sunlight and bugs in the summer, wind and dark in the winter. If you think you'd be interested, make sure you have a long talk with someone that has done it. They're not hard to find.

Day-jobbing

The bulk of us work regular jobs. Sure, there are retirees around, living off of their pensions, but a quick glance of the local neighborhood looks a lot like the rest of America when it comes to employment: teacher, nurse, pilot, security guard, mechanic, fisherman, firefighter, electrician, and so on. Some drive 40 or 45 minutes each way to work. Some work a little closer. The commutes are kind of long in some ways, but far preferable compared to commutes of similar length found farther south. I only drive 25 minutes (each way) for work, but I also have a beautiful drive. I come across no more than 10 other drivers on the road during that whole time—usually it's less than five.

While it may seem like a chore to have to work a day job in order to finance an off-grid lifestyle in rural Alaska, it's a blessing in disguise—it forces us to go out and be with others. We meet new people. We make friends. Connections. We build our own little communities. The relationships are what keep us here. When people leave to go back to the lower 48, they often cite the isolation as one of the main reasons. But they don't *have* to be isolated. They can be integrated, but they choose not to be. They try to live here but still socialize down there. They spend all their time on social media or on the phone, wishing it weren't so hard to visit their friends and family.

To make it work, you must embrace your new home. That means spending time looking at the sunset through your own eyes, not through the camera on your phone, waiting to post the picture online so that everyone you left behind can see how awesome you are now that you live in Alaska. That means investing time in getting to know new people. Your friends back home aren't going to come check on you when that blizzard blows through. They're not going to bring you a moose roast because they don't have enough room in their own freezer for all of that meat. They're not going to teach you how to sharpen your chainsaw. Your old friends will only make you long for a time that can no longer be. They will make you long for a person you no longer are. If you still *are* that person you were trying to leave behind, you will eventually go back to find that person. You will leave. But if you are ready to become new, then become new. You won't make it if you don't grab on with both hands, and that requires letting go of everything else.

About the Author

Jon Crocker lives off-grid on the southern Kenai Peninsula with his wife, children, and pets. In his spare time, he plays music, writes, and develops nearby properties to make them more compatible with sustainable off-grid living. He had a BA in Geography (Environmental Studies), a Master's in Educational Technology, and is working on an EdD in Educational Technology.

He has previously published essays and short stories in various magazines and journals and self-published a novel under a pseudonym. Upcoming works (in progress) include *A Consumer's Guide to Environmentalism* (a no-nonsense look at problems with the modern environmental movement and real solutions to the actual issues), *A Better Robot* (an examination of the ways in which social programming influences our lives and our world), *A Kass'aq Comes and Goes* (an account of two years spent as a teacher in a remote Native village in Alaska), and *Patients* (a novel based on the relativistic nature of sanity). He is also an associate member of the International Society for Philosophical Enquiry.

Other books by Jon Crocker

A Better Robot
A Consumer's Guide to Environmentalism
A Kass'aq Comes and Goes
Patients

Connect with Jon Crocker

http://www.joncrocker.guru

Printed in Great Britain
by Amazon

33716734R00106